Recently, the role of courts has changed dramatically. Not only do courts now have to decide cases between parties, they also often have to choose between competing fundamental values. Judges may have to balance the potentially conflicting interests of human life and human dignity; freedom of speech and the right of privacy; or free trade and the protection of the environment. The courts may have to circumscribe freedom of religion, and decide when religious dress may be worn.

With the non-specialist in mind, and starting from the basic notion of the rule of law, this book explores how judges can and should address such issues. Both the European Convention on Human Rights and the European Union often play a decisive role, and the book points out both the advantages and the difficulties posed by this. Above all, it seeks to promote a more informed debate.

SIR FRANCIS JACOBS, KCMG, QC is Professor of Law at King's College London. Between October 1988 and January 2006 he was Advocate General at the European Court of Justice. Prior to that, he was Director of the Centre of European Law at King's College London from 1981 to 1988, and Professor of European Law in the University of London from 1974 to 1988. He was also in practice at the English Bar, and appeared frequently as Queen's Counsel at the European Court of Justice. He is a Bencher of the Middle Temple.

THE SOVEREIGNTY OF LAW: THE EUROPEAN WAY

By FRANCIS G. JACOBS

Professor of Law, King's College London
and Jean Monnet Professor

Formerly Advocate General, Court of Justice of the European
Communities (1988–2006)

CAMBRIDGE
UNIVERSITY PRESS

CAMBRIDGE UNIVERSITY PRESS
Cambridge, New York, Melbourne, Madrid, Cape Town, Singapore, São Paulo

Cambridge University Press
The Edinburgh Building, Cambridge, CB2 8RU, UK

Published in the United States of America by Cambridge University Press, New York

www.cambridge.org
Information on this title: www.cambridge.org/9780521703857

First published 2007

Printed in the United Kingdom at the University Press, Cambridge

A catalogue record for this publication is available from the British Library

ISBN   978-0-521-87887-6 hardback
ISBN   978-0-521-70385-7 paperback

CONTENTS

The Hamlyn Trust owes its existence today to the will of the late Miss Emma Warburton Hamlyn of Torquay, who died in 1941 at the age of 80. She came of an old and well-known Devon family. Her father, William Bussell Hamlyn, practised in Torquay as a solicitor and J.P. for many years, and it seems likely that Miss Hamlyn founded the trust in his memory. Emma Hamlyn was a woman of strong character, intelligent and cultured, well-versed in literature, music and art, and a lover of her country. She travelled extensively in Europe and Egypt, and apparently took considerable interest in the law and ethnology of the countries and cultures that she visited. An account of Miss Hamlyn by Professor Chantal Stebbings of the University of Exeter may be found, under the title 'The Hamlyn Legacy', in volume 42 of the published lectures.

Miss Hamlyn bequeathed the residue of her estate on trust in terms which it seems were her own. The wording was thought to be vague, and the will was taken to the Chancery Division of the High Court, which in November 1948 approved a Scheme for the administration of the trust. Paragraph 3 of the Scheme, which follows Miss Hamlyn's own wording, is as follows:

> The object of the charity is the furtherance by lectures or otherwise among the Common People of the United Kingdom of Great Britain and Northern Ireland of the

knowledge of the Comparative Jurisprudence and
Ethnology of the Chief European countries including the
United Kingdom, and the circumstances of the growth of
such jurisprudence to the Intent that the Common People
of the United Kingdom may realise the privileges which in
law and custom they enjoy in comparison with other
European Peoples and realising and appreciating such
privileges may recognise the responsibilities and
obligations attaching to them.

The Trustees are to include the Vice-Chancellor of the
University of Exeter, representatives of the Universities of
London, Leeds, Glasgow, Belfast and Wales and persons
co-opted. At present there are eight Trustees:

Professor N. Burrows, The University of Glasgow
Professor I.R. Davies, Swansea University
Ms Clare Dyer
Professor K.M. Economides [representing the Vice-Chancellor
    of the University of Exeter] (Chairman)
Professor J. Morison, Queen's University, Belfast
The Rt Hon. Lord Justice Sedley
Professor A. Sherr, University of London
Professor C. Walker, University of Leeds
Clerk: Ms Charlotte Blackwell, University of Exeter

From the outset it was decided that the objects of the Trust
could be best achieved by means of an annual course of public
lectures of outstanding interest and quality by eminent lecturers, and by their subsequent publication and distribution to a
wider audience. The first of the Lectures were delivered by the
Rt Hon. Lord Justice Denning (as he then was) in 1949. Since

then there has been an unbroken series of annual Lectures published until 2005 by Sweet & Maxwell and from 2006 by Cambridge University Press. A complete list of the Lectures may be found on pages ix to xii. In 2005 the Trustees decided to supplement the Lectures with an annual Hamlyn Seminar, normally held at the Institute of Advanced Legal Studies in the University of London, to mark the publication of the Lectures in printed book form. The Trustees have also, from time to time, provided financial support for a variety of projects which, in various ways, have disseminated knowledge or have promoted to a wider public understanding of the law.

This, the 58th series of lectures was delivered by Sir Francis Jacobs, KCMG, QC at the University of Glasgow, Exeter University and King's College London during October 2006. The Board of Trustees would like to record its appreciation to Sir Francis and also to the three University law schools, which generously hosted these Lectures.

February 2007   **KIM ECONOMIDES**
                                 Chairman of the Trustees

This book is addressed, not primarily to the specialist, but to a wider audience. It tackles some basic questions about the role of law, and the courts, in a society ever more complex.

How has the law developed so that it now seems sometimes the final arbiter on social, ethical and political questions?

How does the law respond to these challenges? How far, in particular, can the law reflect changing values? How far can the law influence those values? What part can and should be played by judges?

I have tried to examine these issues in a European context, and in that context I look in particular at human rights, and at the role of the European Union.

In doing so I have a broader aim, which is to promote a more informed debate about European law.

Although European law is well served by specialists, it suffers from a large information deficit among the wider public. Indeed there seems to be more misinformation, even in legal and professional circles, than a genuine attempt to understand it. Both the place of human rights in our society, and the role of the European Union, are subjects of the greatest importance; yet they have become, in part, the playthings of politicians. This is a damaging and dangerous situation.

*   *   *   *   *   *   *

I am grateful to the Hamlyn Trustees for the invitation to deliver the Hamlyn Lectures on which this book is based. Professor Kim Economides, chairman of the trustees (and a former student of mine), has been exceptionally helpful and encouraging.

My thanks also for the hospitality received at the University of Glasgow, the University of Exeter and King's College London where the lectures were delivered: in particular to Noreen Burrows, to John and Jean Usher and to Raymond Plant and Piet Eeckhout respectively. I am grateful also to Cambridge University Press, and in particular to Finola O'Sullivan for her constant patience and encouragement.

My greatest debt is to my wife, Susan.

Francis G. Jacobs

1

Introduction

The functions of the law seem to have developed dramatically since the days of Miss Emma Hamlyn.

What I seek to show in this book is that many fundamental choices for society are now made, and probably have to be made, not by the legislature, not by the executive, but by the courts. This requires the courts not merely to apply existing legal rules, but to develop the law. In doing so, the courts will necessarily be making value choices, and often balancing competing values, especially where they are confronted with conflicts between them.

For example, in the moral sphere, acute problems arise on the ostensibly sacrosanct right to life: what is its scope? The duty to protect and respect human life may conflict with our conceptions of human dignity. What then should be the response of the courts to the issue of euthanasia?

Many examples of competing values have their origin in the idea of fundamental rights. Especially over the past fifty years, it has become widely accepted in Europe that the protection of fundamental human rights is a principal function of the courts. But often fundamental rights are not, despite the language sometimes used, absolute and unqualified. Freedom of speech may conflict with the right to privacy; currently, there is vital debate about the limits on the fundamental right to practise a religion. So the courts, necessarily, have to strike the balance.

In the sphere of economic policy, we need again to seek to balance competing values: we need to consider, for example, how to reconcile free trade with employment protection, or with protection of the environment. Here too, as we shall see, the courts have to take a leading role.

Choices between competing values thus have to be made by the courts. But where do the values come from – in an increasingly multicultural and pluralist society? What role do values play, and should they play, in shaping the law? And does the law, in turn, have a role in shaping values?

In the past, it was assumed that fundamental decisions were made by a sovereign ruler, and the rules applied by the courts.

In recent years, as final decisions have become more complex, as rules have been shown to be flexible, as principles have emerged to qualify the strict application of rules, so sovereignty seems in some areas to have passed to the courts, and we can speak, if not of the sovereignty of judges, then perhaps of the sovereignty of law. Hence the title of this book.

The theme raises many issues. Some of them, of course, can only be outlined in this book, but they will, I hope, encourage interest in, and debate on, issues of much importance for our society.

Let me then, I hope as an appetizer, outline some of the questions which arise:

1. Is it desirable that courts should have this role? And how far is this role increasingly inevitable?

2. What are the advantages of courts taking final decisions on these issues? What are the difficulties, and what are the dangers?

3. How do courts take their decisions? How far are they, and how far should they be, influenced by existing social values? How far does the law, in turn, influence and help to form social values?

4. At what level should courts take these decisions: how far at the national level, how far at the European level, how far at the global level? To what extent can European answers be given? How much can we learn from other European systems? Or even seek global answers? To what extent should courts look at the experience of courts elsewhere in the world?

These questions arise from the changing functions of law, as the courts have often found themselves to be the ultimate arbiter where goals or values conflict.

In some legal systems this is by no means a novel theme. In the United States, in particular, it has long been taken for granted, and especially for the US Supreme Court. The debates in the United States are rather about the processes of reasoning by which courts should reach, and justify, their decisions: should they, for example, seek to determine the 'original intent' of the US Constitution and seek to give effect to that? Or should they treat the Constitution rather as an evolving instrument, to be adapted to changing circumstances and to changing values?

In the United Kingdom, by contrast, the role of the courts in determining or shaping policy seems rather new.

Historically the most important issue was perhaps the issue of sovereignty – or, in effect, whether the 'sovereign' was, by apparent contradiction, subject to any legal limitations.

Sovereignty

For our purposes, sovereignty can be regarded, historically, as having two aspects: international and internal. In the West, and in particular in Europe, there emerged after the Middle Ages the concept of independent, 'sovereign' States: countries which were not subject to legal rules in their dealings with each other, other than the most basic rules which they could be deemed to have accepted voluntarily. International law, which regulated the behaviour of States, was confined to 'customary' law and treaties. Customary law was limited to rudimentary principles which simply reflected the existing practice of States: for example, the principle that treaties must be observed (*pacta sunt servanda*). Treaties were pacts, or agreements, which the State had concluded voluntarily and by which it was bound by its own consent.

While States were sovereign in their international relations, it was also assumed that within each State there was a 'sovereign' law-maker, more or less unlimited by law.

Whatever may have been the case in the past, it seems clear that sovereignty is no longer a viable concept for explaining either the role of the State in international affairs or the internal arrangements of a modern State.

Internationally, it is not viable on the political level: no State today, even the United States, is able to act independently. Nor is it viable legally: all States actually accept today the

4

constraints of international law, although they may differ about what it requires.

Internally, the traditional concept is equally defunct. Partly, this is a consequence of the previous point: the powers of the State, internally also, are limited by international constraints. But sovereignty is no longer a useful model even where there are no external limits on domestic action. Politically, it has been replaced by some form of the separation of powers; often, with powers divided between legislature, executive and judiciary. Legally, it is difficult, if not impossible, to identify today a State in which a 'sovereign' legislature is not subject to legal limitations on the exercise of its powers.

Moreover, sovereignty is incompatible, both internationally and internally, with another concept which also has a lengthy history, but which today is widely regarded as a paramount value: the rule of law.

The rule of law

The notion of the rule of law also has a long and fascinating history.

The notion that there is a basic or fundamental law (confusingly sometimes known as a higher law) can be traced back for many centuries. The essential idea is that the ordinary laws, even those made by the 'sovereign', are subject to fundamental law, and can therefore be held invalid if they transgress it.

If laws which conflict with the fundamental law are invalid, the question then of course arises: by whom can the laws be held invalid? The most prominent illustration again comes, historically, from the US system, in the famous Supreme Court case of *Marbury* v. *Madison* in 1803.[1] The US Constitution contained no provision for judicial review of legislation enacted by its supreme legislature, the US Congress. But Chief Justice Marshall, finding a conflict between a statute enacted by the US Congress and the Constitution, considered it 'the essence of judicial duty' to follow the Constitution.

This was a leading milestone on the road to what is today called 'constitutionalism': the idea, found in those systems which accept judicial review of legislation, that the constitution – or equivalent constitutional principles – is the fundamental law which entitles the courts to set aside even the laws enacted by democratic legislatures.

Judicial review of the constitutionality of legislation has a dual justification in the US system. First, there is the notion of the Constitution as the supreme law, so that its rules prevail over ordinary legislation. Second, there is the federal system, under which powers are divided between the US Congress and the State legislatures, each being the supreme legislature (subject to the ultimate control of the courts) within its own field of competence.

In turn, such a federal system almost inevitably, it would seem, comports two consequences. First, because the separate legislatures are coequal, there is no true 'sovereign' to be located within the system. Second, there is a need for an independent system of adjudication, to resolve disputes over the respective competences of the 'central' legislature and the

---

[1] *Marbury* v. *Madison* 5 US (1 Cranch) 136 (1803).

State legislatures. That points to the need for a court with an appropriate 'constitutional' jurisdiction.

In the United Kingdom, by contrast, there have traditionally been no legal limits on the sovereignty of Parliament: even today, the only exceptions are those entailed by membership of the European Union. There is otherwise no judicial review of Acts of Parliament; indeed the term 'judicial review' has been expropriated by administrative law to refer exclusively to review of the executive – a government minister, for example, or a local authority where it is alleged that they have acted unlawfully; and the expression 'judicial review' is now used as a technical term to denote the application to the court for a remedy for such unlawful administrative action.

The meaning of the rule of law

The rule of law is today universally recognized as a fundamental value. But there is not universal agreement about what it means. Nor is there agreement about how it can be reconciled with other, competing values: notably, with the requirements of democratic government.

There are two aspects of the rule of law: formal and substantive. Formally, the principle requires that the exercise of power – and thus all acts of the public authorities – is, with narrow exceptions, subject to review by the courts to ensure that the exercise was authorized by law. This aspect of the rule of law is also known as the principle of legality.

I had intended to say a good deal, in this introductory chapter, about the evolution of the substance of the rule of law and its significance today. But on reflection, I prefer, if I can put it that way, to let it speak for itself. What the rule of law involves and requires will, I hope, emerge very clearly from this book.

It will certainly become clear that it cannot coexist with traditional conceptions of sovereignty.

What I hope should result from this book is that the rule of law embodies certain values which seem, at least in Europe, widely accepted as essential to modern social and political life; and that we shall be able to identify some of those values.

But we shall look also at other areas where fundamental value choices have to be made by the courts.

The scope of our subject is therefore broad, but that may be appropriate for the Hamlyn Lectures. And we may even find that there are links that can be made between the values embodied in the rule of law and other fundamental social and ethical values which the courts have to take into account.

Finally, it is appropriate, today, to look at the United Kingdom in its European setting. Both the European Convention on Human Rights and European Community law have given UK law a new dimension – as was anticipated by Leslie Scarman in his 1974 Hamlyn Lectures 'English Law – The New Dimension'. I will suggest that the European dimension has been, and remains, a valuable input, reinforcing the fundamental values of English law.

2

The rule of law in Europe

The two European systems: an outline

The two European systems I have referred to in the previous chapter – the European Convention on Human Rights and European Community law – are very different from one another in their substance, and they operate in very different ways. But each, as we shall see, has an important role in reinforcing the rule of law; moreover, by a combination of chance and design, they complement one another.

To summarize in the briefest terms: the European Convention on Human Rights, first conceived in 1950 with much input from the United Kingdom, is binding on the currently forty-six member States of the Council of Europe. The European Court of Human Rights, based in Strasbourg, hears cases brought mainly by individuals, occasionally by corporations, exceptionally even by governments, alleging breach of the human rights guaranteed by the Convention. Cases can be taken to Strasbourg only after all domestic channels of redress have failed. The judgment of the Court, if it finds a breach, is binding on the State against which it is given, and the Court may award compensation.

The European Community, which had its origins also in 1950, now the European Union, is a union of currently twenty-seven Member States. It was initially set up with primarily economic functions, but with political aspirations. It now has competence in many fields, and in most of those fields Community legislation is applied within the Member States. In some areas Community legislation is directly applicable within the Member State, side by side with domestic law; in other areas Community legislation is transposed by national Parliaments into domestic law. It is applied by the domestic courts.

Because Community law (both Community legislation and the Community Treaties) is largely applied within the Member States by the national authorities, and must be applied uniformly throughout the Member States if it is to be effective, the final word on its interpretation rests with the Court of Justice of the European Communities, based in Luxembourg. The European Court of Justice (ECJ), as it is often known, has a wide jurisdiction. In the development of the law, the most important head of jurisdiction enables it to give rulings, at the request of national courts, on the meaning and effect of Community law.

National courts at all levels are free to make references, and when doing so they suspend their own proceedings to await the answers to the questions they refer. National courts of last instance are obliged, under the EC Treaty, to make a reference, if a decision on the question of Community law is necessary to enable them to give judgment.

This reference procedure can be contrasted with the Strasbourg system, where the route to the European Court of Human Rights is open only after all 'domestic remedies', as they are termed, have been exhausted. But the requirement to exhaust domestic remedies is appropriate to the Strasbourg Court, which is essentially an international court – although one with a remarkable jurisdiction – and a court which does not seek to unify the law, but rather to set a minimum European standard.

In contrast, the procedure for references to the ECJ from the national courts is particularly appropriate to the more integrated Community system: in this system, Community law is an integral part of the internal law of each Member State, and is to be applied uniformly throughout the Community; and the national courts of the Member States can also be regarded as Community courts.

Because the rulings of the ECJ are given before the national court gives judgment, they are called 'preliminary rulings'; but they are often decisive for the outcome of the case. The rulings given by the ECJ are binding on all national courts: otherwise they would not achieve their purpose. They may therefore decide many other potential disputes over the same provisions, and this is one of their most valuable functions.

But the system of preliminary rulings (or 'preliminary references') also makes it possible for the ECJ and the national court to have what is often called a 'dialogue'. It is the national court which is the direct interlocutor of the ECJ. The national court can explain its concerns, and its national law. In this way, the various systems of national law have had a great influence on the development of Community law. We shall see illustrations of ways in which this process has been mutually beneficial to Community law and national law, and has contributed to reinforcing the rule of law.

Before giving its ruling, the ECJ will hear the parties to the case, and also the Member States and Community institutions that wish to take part. Where the question of law is new, the Court will also have the benefit of the Opinion of an

Advocate General, a member of the Court whose special function is to deliver an opinion designed to assist the judges in the resolution of the case. The Court should in consequence be in a unique position to take a considered view on the solution of the case and on what the development of the law requires.

'The European way'

In a typical and brilliant passage, the great English judge Lord Denning (who was also the first Hamlyn lecturer) contrasted the EEC Treaty with the character of English law and legislation. In one of the first cases where English courts were confronted with the Treaty, he declared, in his own inimitable style:[1]

> The treaty is quite unlike any of the enactments to which we have become accustomed . . . It lays down general principles. It expresses its aim and purposes. All in sentences of moderate length and commendable style. But it lacks precision. It uses words and phrases without defining what they mean. An English lawyer would look for an interpretation clause, but he would look in vain. There is none. All the way through the treaty there are gaps and lacunae. These have to be filled in by the judges . . . It is the European way.

This passage does indeed graphically express some of the great differences between the EEC Treaty and UK legislation: and indeed between UK legislation and the European Convention on Human Rights, although Lord Denning was not addressing that.

[1] *Bulmer* v. *Bollinger* [1974] Ch 401, at p. 425.

(The explicit contrast between 'English' and 'European' need not, I think, be taken to suggest that England is somewhere else than in Europe. It is simply a convenient shorthand – still convenient today. Moreover the two legal systems do remain in some ways separate: the relation between national law and European Community law is, as we have seen, to some extent a matter of two separate systems coexisting within the Member States.)

But some qualifications of Lord Denning's view are appropriate, at least today.

First, the contrast with the EEC Treaty is striking because the Treaty is, as we shall see, in part comparable to a Constitution for the European Community. If the United Kingdom had a written constitution, that would necessarily, as a constitution, share the features of the Treaty as described by Lord Denning, and British judges would have to apply its broad and imprecise provisions. This is indeed the position today in almost every country and almost every legal system in the world.

Second, despite the abundance, perhaps the excess, of legislation, in both Community and English law, both systems are still to a large extent – as is the European Convention – a case-law system, in which the decisions of the courts play a leading role. Again, we shall see many examples of this.

Third, as Lord Denning also pointed out, the gaps in the Treaty have to be filled, not only by the judges, but also by Community legislation: he refers to regulations and directives. Much Community legislation does not match his description: it is rather detailed; it often contains definitions and interpretation clauses. The contrast between UK legislation and Community legislation, as distinct from the Treaty, is less great.

Fourth, English courts have in recent years increasingly taken a more 'European' approach to the interpretation of domestic UK legislation even where it has no European content. They look rather less at the literal wording, and rather more at the aim and purposes of the legislation. In their approach to legislation, they are more ready to apply general principles, such as the principles of proportionality and human rights. There are still differences between the approach of English judges and the approach of the European Courts. But they are now often differences of degree, not differences of principle. This is just one, rather positive, example of a process of convergence between different legal systems in Europe.

To some extent, in our day, English courts are following 'the European way'.

The two European systems and the rule of law

In the following chapters we shall explore some of the contributions which these two European systems make to reinforcing the rule of law. But it may be useful to make at the outset some general comments.

I would suggest that there are three principal ways in which they can have this effect.

First, they provide an additional remedy, which is not available under the domestic law, and which may prove highly effective.

This is most obviously true of the European Convention on Human Rights, under which the Strasbourg

Court may provide a remedy precisely where there is no 'domestic remedy'. Innumerable examples could be taken.

European Community law can also provide a remedy, notably where a Community institution acts unlawfully. Here the national courts have no jurisdiction, but the Court of First Instance and, on appeal, the ECJ have proved effective guardians of the rights of individuals and corporations, even if their access to the Court – their standing to bring proceedings – is still too restricted.[2]

Second, the two systems can improve the domestic systems by requiring that a remedy be available within that system.

A classic illustration under the Convention system is the *Golder* case.[3] Here the issue was whether a convicted prisoner had the right, under Article 6(1) of the Convention, to take legal proceedings to clear his name. The UK authorities had effectively refused him permission to sue. Article 6(1) of the Convention provides:

> In the determination of his civil rights and obligations . . .
> everyone is entitled to a fair and public hearing within a
> reasonable time by an independent and impartial tribunal
> established by law.

Does that provision guarantee only certain procedural rights once a court is seised of a case: or does it also guarantee a right of access to a court? The Strasbourg Court, to answer that question, relied on, among other things, the notion of the rule of law, which is referred to in the preamble to the Convention.

[2] See Paul Craig, *EU Administrative Law* (Oxford, 2006), pp. 331 ff.
[3] *Golder* v. *United Kingdom* (1975) 1 EHRR 524.

The Court held that the provision guarantees a right (although not an unlimited right) of access to a court:[4]

> . . . one can scarcely conceive of the rule of law without there being a possibility of access to the courts . . . The principle whereby a civil claim must be capable of being submitted to a judge ranks as one of the universally recognised fundamental principles of law; the same is true of international law which forbids the denial of justice. Article 6 (1) must be read in the light of these principles.

More generally, Article 13 sets out the requirements of the Convention to provide an effective remedy for breach of the Convention rights themselves:

> Everyone whose rights and freedoms as set forth in this Convention are violated shall have an effective remedy before a national authority notwithstanding that the violation has been committed by persons acting in an official capacity.

For its part, European Community law also insists on the availability of a remedy in national law for breach of a Community law right. The right to an effective remedy before the national courts has been recognized by the ECJ as a general principle of law; the principle is sometimes described as the right to judicial protection. Remedies and procedural rules provided for by national law will be scrutinized by the ECJ to ensure that they do not unduly impede the effective exercise of Community rights: if they do so, the national court must not apply them.

---

[4] *Ibid.* at paras. 34–5.

Third, the European systems can influence the development of national law. As we shall see, there is a two-way process at work, especially in relation to EC law: principles of national law may have a positive influence on the development of EC law; conversely, EC law may have a beneficial influence on the development of national law. This is one of the consequences of the 'dialogue' between the ECJ and the national courts; and it exists also, as we shall see, with the European Court of Human Rights.

In these various ways, the European systems – which we shall now look at a little more closely – strengthen the rule of law in Europe.

3

The European Convention on Human Rights and the rule of law

The European Convention on Human Rights[1] was drawn up under the auspices of the Council of Europe, the first of the European organizations seeking to build a new European order from the rubble of the Second World War.

The Council of Europe was established in 1949, before even the first of the European Communities. It was symbolically located in Strasbourg, a city which had frequently changed hands between France and Germany in a series of bloody wars, culminating in the two World Wars of the twentieth century.

The preamble to the Statute of the Council of Europe refers to shared spiritual and moral values. The contracting States reaffirm 'their devotion to the spiritual and moral values which are the common heritage of their peoples and the true source of individual freedom, political liberty and the rule of law, principles which form the basis of all genuine democracy'.

---

[1] The full title of the Convention is: Convention for the Protection of Human Rights and Fundamental Freedoms. The full title is often stated inaccurately, in various ways. It is even given inaccurately in the Treaty on European Union (Article 6(2)) – where the Convention is referred to as the *European* Convention for the Protection of Human Rights and Fundamental Freedoms. The inaccurate title therefore permeates some of the case-law of the European Court of Justice. In ordinary use it seems preferable to use the title by which the Convention is universally known – the European Convention on Human Rights.

By Article 3 of the Statute, every member State of the Council of Europe 'must accept the principles of the rule of law and of the enjoyment by all persons within its jurisdiction of human rights and fundamental freedoms'. By Articles 7 and 8 of the Statute, a member State which seriously violates Article 3 may be suspended from the Council of Europe, and ultimately expelled. These provisions had no parallel in the history of international organizations.

The European Convention on Human Rights

The European Convention on Human Rights, adopted in Rome on 4 November 1950, was drafted in the wake of the Second World War and the Holocaust. It was conceived in part as an 'early warning system' to prevent States from lapsing into totalitarianism. It set out the fundamental rights and freedoms that States were required to secure to everyone within their jurisdiction. Moreover it provided, for the first time in the history of international law, an enforcement system: States were subject to the jurisdiction of an international court for the protection of the human rights of their subjects and of all those subject to their jurisdiction.

The rights protected by the Convention, set out in Section I of the Convention, were those fundamental rights regarded as both essential and uncontroversial: they included most of the basic civil and political rights contained in the Universal Declaration of Human Rights – with the difference, of course, that the European Convention provided not merely a declaration but a system of judicial enforcement. The Convention guarantees include the right to life, liberty and security; freedom from torture and inhuman or degrading treatment, slavery, servitude and forced labour; the right to a fair trial; freedom of conscience, of speech and of assembly.

Further rights were added by subsequent Protocols to the Convention: these included property rights and the right to education. The First Protocol also requires States to organize free elections, thus establishing a direct link between human rights and democracy, a link to which we shall return.

The enforcement system consisted of a European Commission of Human Rights and subsequently also, when sufficient States had agreed, a European Court of Human Rights. There was an option for a State to accept the competence of the Commission to receive applications by individuals (rather than States) against that State, and to accept the jurisdiction of the European Court of Human Rights.

The Convention has proved extraordinarily effective, not least because it could be implemented progressively. Initially, States could join the Council of Europe without being required to sign the Convention. They could subsequently sign the Convention with a view to ratifying, and thus being bound by, the Convention. And they could later ratify the Convention without thereby accepting the system of supervision which it introduced: the jurisdiction of the European Court of Human Rights, or the competence of the European Commission of Human Rights to accept petitions from individuals. Only very gradually did the States accept these mechanisms: a turning-point was reached when the United Kingdom accepted in 1966 the right of individual petition.

The United Kingdom and the Convention

The United Kingdom has played a leading role throughout the history of the Convention, and its contribution to it has been immense. Its representatives took an active part in the drafting of the Convention. Indeed the Convention text, although based on many sources, including the Universal Declaration of Human Rights, could be regarded as embodying, in an entirely novel form in terms of English law, and in lucid and straightforward language, the fundamental principles of English law on civil liberties and the freedom of the individual.

The United Kingdom was also the first State to ratify the Convention, although there was no thought, at that stage, of adopting the optional steps of accepting the jurisdiction of the European Commission and, after it was established, the European Court of Human Rights.

In the decolonization process of the 1960s, the United Kingdom adopted the Convention, not as part of its own internal law – that was to come much later – but as a fundamental part of the Constitutions of the newly independent States of the Commonwealth.

The UK's decision to accept in 1966 the jurisdiction of the European Commission and the Court of Human Rights can be seen as a defining moment in the life of the Convention. It was unexpected and unheralded. The decision came without discussion in the United Kingdom. It was unexpected, although welcome, in Europe. At that time, the optional jurisdiction clauses had been accepted only by some of the smaller countries in Europe, and by only one of the larger countries, Germany, which had had the most obvious historical reasons to accept the Strasbourg jurisdiction. The Strasbourg system was little known in other countries. The acceptance of the system by the United Kingdom helped to put the system on the map.

Development of the Strasbourg system

Since then, the Strasbourg system has been extraordinarily successful in promoting respect for human rights. Moreover it proved possible to improve the system of protection: notably so as to give the individual applicant the right of action before the Court, rather than seizure of the Court being confined to States and the Commission of Human Rights. The story is indeed a remarkable one, without precedent or parallel in international affairs. And it is particularly striking that these developments took place in Europe, where State sovereignty had the longest history, and might have been thought most strongly entrenched.

Furthermore, once all members of the Council of Europe had voluntarily accepted the system, they succeeded by unanimous agreement in amending the Convention so as to merge the Commission with the Court, to establish the Court on a full-time basis and to provide that adherence to the Convention entails automatic and permanent acceptance of the Court's jurisdiction. The Eleventh Protocol, which introduced these profound changes, entered into force on 1 November 1998.

As the Council of Europe has grown to almost fifty nations, acceptance of the Convention has also become, in practical and political terms although not by law, a necessary condition of membership. This has had one unfortunate consequence, in that political pressure to admit States to the Council of Europe has resulted in States acceding to the Convention when they were not truly ready to accept the commitments required by it.

Acceptance of the Convention is also a precondition of membership of the European Union, which as we shall see is itself now a body firmly based on respect for human rights.

Indeed the Convention can be regarded as a touchstone of respect for human rights.

Moreover the Convention has been accepted as forming part of the domestic, internal law of many of the States parties to it. Progressively the Convention has been incorporated into domestic law – sometimes by States' own courts' interpretation of their national constitution, sometimes by specific domestic legislation – and has thereby been given internal legal effect in almost all the member States of the Council of Europe. This internal effect, enabling the Convention to be invoked in the domestic courts, has obvious advantages.

The Convention and United Kingdom law

Despite having ratified the Convention as long ago as 1950, and accepting the jurisdiction of the Commission and the Court in 1966, it was not until 1998 that the United Kingdom, with the Human Rights Act 1998, incorporated most of the Convention rights into domestic law.

It might have been possible for the domestic courts to take greater account of the Convention without such incorporation. But the English courts took the view, despite valiant efforts by occasional judicial decisions and academic writings,[2] that so long as the Convention was not incorporated into English law, they could not give effect to the Convention. The disappointed litigant would have to resort to Strasbourg to vindicate his or her rights.

However, because the Convention required as a pre-condition the 'exhaustion of domestic remedies', the Strasbourg applicant would normally have to show, before the merits of the complaint could even be considered in Strasbourg, that all domestic avenues of appeal, up to and including the highest courts, had been tried and failed.

To be able to rely upon the Convention in the domestic courts makes obvious sense. It may often avoid the need to trouble the Court of Human Rights. But in the United Kingdom the idea met strong opposition. The United Kingdom was the only State party to the Convention in which the courts could not apply either the Convention itself or an equivalent domestic Bill of Rights.

Moreover the United Kingdom was one of very few countries in the world without a Bill of Rights. It had exported the Convention, as we have seen, to its former colonies. Commonwealth States had drawn up their own Bills of Rights, in which the European Convention had some influence. Notable examples are the Canadian Charter of Rights and Freedoms and the New Zealand Bill of Rights. A rare example of a State without a Bill of Rights is Australia.

---

[2] See notably Murray Hunt, *Using Human Rights Law in English Courts* (Hart Publishing, Oxford, 1997).

In the United Kingdom the cause of incorporating the Convention long remained a very minority interest. But it was promoted by a few outstanding lawyers: by Leslie Scarman (notably in his 1974 Hamlyn Lectures 'English Law – The New Dimension') and by Anthony Lester.

More recently, in the 1990s, but no less remarkably, the cause was accepted and promoted by senior English judges, not least by successive Lords Chief Justice: Peter Taylor, Tom Bingham and Harry Woolf.

The deed was finally done, with the impetus of Lord Chancellor Irvine, with the enactment of the Human Rights Act 1998.

The Human Rights Act 1998

The Human Rights Act 1998 made two fundamental changes in UK law. First, it incorporated into English law, with effect from 2 October 2000, most of the rights provided for by the European Convention (and its First and Sixth Protocols). The 'Convention rights', as they are termed, are set out in a Schedule to the Act. The Act provides, among other things:

> It is unlawful for a public authority to act in a way which is incompatible with a Convention right (section 6(1)).

Second, the Human Rights Act introduced an ingenious combination of solutions for possible conflicts between fundamental rights and the sovereignty of Parliament.

It seeks in the first place to avoid such conflicts by requiring the UK courts to construe all legislation, both primary and subordinate, consistently with Convention rights where it is possible to do so: such legislation must, by section 3 of the Act, be read and given effect in a way which is compatible with Convention rights 'so far as it is possible to do so'.

It is said that the model for this formula was the New Zealand Bill of Rights Act 1990. That Act provides by section 6: 'Wherever an enactment can be given a meaning that is consistent with the rights and freedoms contained in this Bill of Rights, that meaning shall be preferred to any other meaning.' It is also said that the formula used in the British Act, 'so far as it is possible to do so', is slightly stronger.[3]

It is sometimes overlooked, however, that the British formula bears a close resemblance to the proposition formulated in the domain of European Community law by the European Court of Justice (ECJ) concerning the obligation of national courts to interpret national legislation consistently with Community legislation in the form of directives. The two main forms of Community legislation are different in this respect. Community *regulations* are, according to the Treaty, directly applicable in all Member States; and they therefore prevail over any conflicting domestic legislation. Community *directives* normally require to be transposed into the law of the Member States by domestic legislation. The ECJ has accordingly had to consider the scope of the national court's duty to interpret national legislation consistently with Community directives. The ECJ ruled in the *Marleasing* case in 1990 that:[4]

---

[3] See Wade and Forsyth, *Administrative Law* (Oxford University Press, Oxford, 8th edition 2000), p. 189.

[4] *Marleasing SA v. La Comercial Internacional de Alimentacion SA* [1990] ECR I-4135, at para. 9.

> . . . in applying national law, whether the provisions in
> question were adopted before or after the directive, the
> national court called upon to interpret it is required to do
> so, as far as possible, in the light of the wording and the
> purpose of the directive.

The effect is, in practice, that national legislation must be interpreted consistently with directives unless it is impossible to do so because the national legislation flatly contradicts the directive. The obligation of the UK courts under the Human Rights Act 1998 uses very similar language ('as far as possible' compared with 'so far as it is possible to do so'); and it can be understood in the same way. Indeed it would be appropriate and convenient for the same approach to be taken to two European sources of law.

But what if there is a clear conflict between UK legislation and Convention rights, so that the courts cannot construe UK legislation consistently with the Convention? For that event, the Human Rights Act 1998 introduces a wholly new mechanism into the UK 'Constitution' – a mechanism which can perhaps be traced back to a proposal of the great international lawyer Hersch Lauterpacht.

Where the courts (in any event, the higher courts: the High Court and above) find a conflict between the rights protected by the Human Rights Act 1998 and another Act of Parliament, they can make a 'declaration of incompatibility'.

Such a declaration has the effect that an Act found to conflict with the Convention is not overridden, and cannot be disapplied by the courts, as would be the case under directly applicable European Community law. Instead, if the court makes a declaration of incompatibility, the Act of Parliament found to conflict with the Convention can be amended in Parliament by a relatively straightforward procedure in order to remove the defect identified by the British court.

Thus, in the event of a declaration of incompatibility, the Government may take remedial action. Under section 10(2) of the Human Rights Act 1998, if a Minister of the Crown considers that there are compelling reasons for proceeding under this section, he or she may by order make such amendments to the legislation as he or she considers necessary to remove the incompatibility.

The 'remedial order' must first be laid in draft before Parliament for sixty days and approved by resolution of each House.

In addition, all new legislation is subjected before its enactment to special scrutiny by a joint committee of both Houses of Parliament, assisted by specialist legal advisers, to check its compatibility with the Convention.

When the Bill goes through Parliament, the Government must make a statement on its compatibility with the Convention rights. By section 19 of the Act, a Minister of the Crown in charge of a Bill in either House of Parliament must, before Second Reading of the Bill, either make a statement to the effect that in his or her view the provisions of the Bill are compatible with the Convention rights (a 'statement of compatibility'); or make a statement to the effect that, although he is unable to make a statement of compatibility, the Government nevertheless wishes the House to proceed with the Bill.

The statement must be in writing, and must be published in such manner as the Minister considers appropriate.

The impact of the Human Rights Act 1998

What then has been the impact of the Human Rights Act 1998? It is now possible, after some years of experience of the Act, to take stock of its effects. Since the Act was passed the situation has been transformed: in ways sometimes predictable, sometimes surprising.

The UK courts – with the assistance of special training courses provided for the judges at all levels – have, by and large, adjusted very successfully to the requirements of the Convention.

The predicted inundation of the courts with grievances, real and imaginary, has not materialized. True, the tabloid Press seeks to suggest the reverse, and speaks of the development of a 'human rights culture' in the wrong sense, with supposed human rights being invoked, and applied, to no good purpose. But this is not the perception of informed observers, and notably of the judges themselves.

In fact a great deal of nonsense about the Convention has passed into the media and perhaps into public opinion. There is nothing in the Convention, for example, which requires the rights of offenders, or of persons dangerous to the public, to be preferred to the rights of the innocent citizen. The Government has failed, however, to meet public concerns, and to explain the effects of the Act: perhaps because there is little perceived political advantage to be gained.

In fact the worst of all policies is to debase the concept of human rights. Having finally incorporated the Convention into English law, the Government has a special responsibility to guard its image.

As well as the great advantages of putting English law on a proper footing, with, for the first time, a proper system of human rights protection, a further remarkable development is the valuable body of human rights case-law which the UK courts have built up in the relatively short period since the Human Rights Act 1998 came into force.

Several types of illustration can be given of the contributions made by the English cases.

First, there are leading cases where the courts have found a violation of the human rights protected by the Convention and the Act. One of the leading examples is the 'Belmarsh' case,[5] in which the House of Lords held that the detention without trial of foreign nationals under the Anti-terrorism, Crime and Security Act 2001 was incompatible with human rights.

As might be expected, however, there have been rather few declarations of incompatibility: these require the courts to find, not merely a violation of the Convention, but that an Act of Parliament cannot be construed consistently with the Convention.

Second, the courts have recognized what was not generally apparent: that the Act has had a significant impact on English law going beyond the outcomes of individual cases. It has resulted in no less than a 'constitutional shift'. Traditionally most fundamental rights were not proclaimed by English law. Instead, they were often residual: freedom of expression, for example, existed only to the extent that partic-

---

[5] *A v. Secretary of State for the Home Department* [2005] 2 AC 68.

ular forms of expression were not prohibited or restricted by law.

Now, freedom of expression, and other fundamental rights, are expressed positively: as, in effect, constitutional rights.

Third, one of the most interesting consequences of incorporation of the Convention is that the case-law of the British courts has had an impact also on the case-law of the European Court of Human Rights. In part this was predictable, and indeed was no doubt one of the motives for giving the Convention effect in UK law.

Before the UK courts were able to apply the Convention, the Strasbourg Court in turn found no assistance in the UK courts' judgments. Since the Convention was incorporated into UK law, the carefully reasoned pronouncements of the UK courts on the interpretation and application of the Convention, as mirrored in the Human Rights Act 1998, seem certain to have an influence on the Strasbourg Court.

But the influence has been even stronger than might have been expected. As I found when researching this subject, there have been several cases where the English case-law has persuaded the Strasbourg Court to revise its own previous case-law.

Examples of this situation can be found in several cases decided in Strasbourg after decisions by English courts. The cases concern such diverse matters as the liability in damages of public authorities;[6] the compatibility of UK

---

[6] The *Osman* case-law: *Osman* v. *United Kingdom* (1998) 29 EHRR 245, modified in *Z* v. *United Kingdom* (2001) 34 EHRR 97.

court-martial proceedings with the requirements of a fair trial;[7] and the system of mandatory life sentences.[8] In all three cases the Strasbourg Court, it seems, has, quite remarkably, modified its case-law in response to fully reasoned decisions of the English courts.

The achievements of the Convention, in both estab-lishing jurisprudence on human rights and promoting human rights and democracy across Europe, are immense. It has expanded to include and support new and developing democ-racies. It has greatly strengthened the rule of law across Europe, and can even be said to have contributed significantly to the continued peace and stability of the Continent.[9]

One is therefore bemused by the proposal in some political circles in Britain which envisages the idea of repealing the Human Rights Act 1998 and replacing it with a 'home-grown' Bill of Rights.

First, the European Convention is home-grown in the important sense that it reflects UK law. As we have seen, English lawyers took an active part in the making of the Convention; it reflects the principles of the common law; and the United Kingdom has exported the Convention to its colonies on independence.

---

[7] In *Cooper* v. *United Kingdom* [2003] ECHR 48843/99, the Grand Chamber departed from the judgment of a Chamber in *Morris* v. *United Kingdom* [2002] ECHR 38784/97.

[8] In *Stafford* v. *United Kingdom* (2002) 35 EHRR 1121, the Court modified its judgment in *Wynne* v. *United Kingdom* (1994) 19 EHRR 333.

[9] See Lord Woolf, *Review of the Working Methods of the European Court of Human Rights* (Council of Europe and European Court of Human Rights, Strasbourg, December 2005).

Where the Convention differs – and differs radically – from English law is not by its content, but by its shape and its technique. What the Convention does is to transpose the rules which subsisted in English law into a Bill of Rights. (Although England had a Bill of Rights of 1689, which substantially curtailed the powers of the King, that was not comparable with a modern Bill of Rights.) English law proceeded differently: its development was conditioned by the availability of particular remedies, and by 'forms of action' – the traditional procedures by which claims could be brought before the courts.

Against that background, it makes little sense to talk of replacing the Convention with a British Bill of Rights.

Moreover, there are obvious advantages for the United Kingdom in being part of a shared system: it has advantages for the protection of rights in the United Kingdom itself; and a collective system strengthens the protection of rights, and reinforces the values of democracy and the rule of law, for the whole of Europe, to the benefit of the United Kingdom as well.

There are also the specific advantages of incorporation of the Convention which we have already touched upon, notably that UK courts have the first word in applying the Convention rights – and may have a positive influence on the development of Convention law by the Strasbourg Court.

And what would be the consequences of repealing the Human Rights Act 1998 and introducing a different Bill of Rights, not directly reflecting the Convention? Would we remain parties to the Convention – and so remain subject to the jurisdiction of the Strasbourg Court, but without the benefits of incorporation? What then would be the point of repealing the Act?

Or would we pull out of the Convention system altogether? That would require formal denunciation of the Convention, and would be totally demeaning: the only precedent is the regime of the Greek colonels in the late 1960s. Their practice of torture and other systematic violations of human rights compelled Greece to denounce the Convention to avoid further public disgrace. To denounce the Convention would also entail leaving the Council of Europe; and indeed leaving the European Union.

There is a strand of opinion in the United Kingdom which would, however irrationally, accept those consequences with equanimity or even with delight, although such drastic, even seismic options have never been on the agenda of a mainstream political party.

Informed opinion regards the Convention system as an unprecedentedly effective system for the collective enforcement of human rights in Europe, and indeed as a model for the world.

4

The European Union and the rule of law

The <u>European Union is based on the rule of law to a far</u> greater extent than any previous or contemporary international or transnational organization. The key to the notion of the rule of law is, as we have seen, the <u>reviewability of decisions of public authorities by</u> independent courts; the European Union goes far in recognizing this.

The European Communities – starting with the European Coal and Steel Community in 1950 – were created by law, in the shape of treaties, and endowed with a Court of Justice, whose function, stated in the broadest terms, was to ensure that the law was observed. Moreover, in contrast to other international and transnational courts, the jurisdiction of the European Court of Justice (ECJ) was not optional, but compulsory and automatic.

The <u>ECJ was given a wide jurisdiction</u> – the key to the effectiveness of the Treaties and to the <u>observance of the rule of law.</u>

Among its main functions was, and still is, to ensure the legality of the measures taken by the new institutions created by the Treaties, so that their considerable powers are exercised in accordance with the law. Specifically, the ECJ is to <u>annul any measures where the institutions exceed or misuse their powers, or infringe other essential rules.</u> In practice, any form of substantial <u>wrongdoing,</u> not necessarily requiring fault, is a sufficient ground for <u>annulment.</u> In other words – although this was not an expression used in the Treaties – the Court's function was, and still is, to protect the rule of law.

But it was not only the Community institutions that were to be held to the law. The Member States also were, and are, subject to the jurisdiction of the ECJ. The European Commission, or another Member State, can take the default-ing State before the Court for any infringement of the Treaties or of EC legislation. The Member States are required to comply with any adverse judgment. This jurisdiction has generally been extremely effective. Often the launch, or even the prospect, of proceedings has been sufficient to induce Member States to comply. The proceedings became even more effective under the Treaty on European Union. Under the Treaty as thereby amended, a Member State which fails to comply with a judgment of the Court is liable to have a very substantial fine imposed on it – a sanction introduced at the instigation of the United Kingdom. There is no precedent or equivalent in inter-national law to this system of enforcement.

Thus the rule of law is applicable both to the institu-tions and to the Member States.

A further principal function of the ECJ, apart from these direct challenges, is to rule on questions of Community law referred to it by a court of a Member State. Such references sometimes lead the Court to rule, indirectly rather than directly, on the lawfulness of the acts of institutions or Member States. But the jurisdiction to give these rulings has con-tributed to the rule of law far more broadly. As we shall see, by this mechanism the Court has developed a remarkable body of case-law, including a body of administrative law which seeks to strike an appropriate balance between the public authorities and the individual, and which has even inspired substantial and positive developments in the purely internal law of the Member States.

Thus, although the term 'rule of law' and its counterparts in other Community languages were not used in the Treaties, the rule of law has been effectively guaranteed by the wide jurisdiction conferred on an active and independent court.

The Treaty's only general provision governing the ECJ was perhaps understated; it read:

> The Court of Justice shall ensure that in the interpretation and application of this Treaty the law is observed.

But the English text may be slightly misleading here, reflecting in accordance with the English 'positivist' tradition a strictly formal view of what 'the law' is. On this view, the law is 'positive law', i.e. the law as enacted. Accordingly, law and justice are often distinguished – or even contrasted. In other languages, however, what the law is and what is right or just are less starkly distinguished. Thus in French, German or Italian the terms '*droit*', '*Recht*', '*diritto*' have a broader connotation. Indeed it has even been suggested that the English text might have been closer to them, or to the intended meaning of the provision, if it had stated explicitly that the ECJ shall ensure that the *rule of law* is observed. But the rule of law is only part of what is right, or what is just; and its meaning should not be too far diluted.

It should be added that the establishment in 1989 of the Court of First Instance, created to hear certain actions at first instance with a right of appeal to the ECJ, was intended to improve observance of the rule of law in a very specific sense, namely to 'improve the judicial protection of individual interests'.[1]

The jurisdiction of the Court of First Instance has been progressively extended, and the Treaty (Article 220) now imposes the same fundamental task on both Courts:

> The Court of Justice and the Court of First Instance, each within its jurisdiction, shall ensure that in the interpretation and application of this Treaty the law is observed.

At least an important part of this task is to ensure that *the rule of law* is observed.

The Community legal order

The development of the Community legal order – a new legal system appropriate to the needs of this novel structure – and the role of the ECJ in its creation and development will feature at several points in this book. As might be expected, the Court has played a significant role in the creation of the internal market and in the economic law of the Community: aspects of this are considered in chapter 6.

But beyond that, and less predictably, the ECJ has fashioned the foundations of the Community legal system itself and, as part of that, has developed a system of administrative law, including fundamental principles governing the

---

[1] See the preamble to the Council Decision of 24 October 1988 establishing a Court of First Instance of the European Communities, 88/591/ECSC, EEC, Euratom, OJ L 319, 25.11.1988, p. 1–8.

relations between the public authorities and the individual – principles going to the heart of the rule of law.

A few words must suffice on the foundations of the Community legal system. Here I will limit myself to what seem to me the key notions: the notions of direct effect and primacy, which are specific features of EC law; the jurisdiction of the ECJ; and fundamental principles of law common to modern European systems.

Direct effect

Perhaps the single most significant concept is that of direct effect, laid down for the first time in a judgment delivered by the ECJ in 1963. The question referred to the Court in *van Gend en Loos*[2] was essentially whether a specific Treaty provision could be enforced in the national courts in the face of conflicting national legislation. Here the Court held that the Community constituted a new legal order of international law for the benefit of which the States had limited their sovereign rights, and the subjects of which comprised not only Member States but also their nationals. The Treaty created individual rights which the national courts must protect.

The ruling, although at the time controversial, was crucial to the effectiveness of Community law and indeed to the very existence of the rule of law.

In the first place, it meant that individuals could secure recognition and enforcement of their rights in the national courts.

[2] *Algemene Transport-en Expeditie Onderneming van Gend en Loos NV v. Nederlandse Belastingadministratie* [1963] ECR 1.

Second, the principle of direct effect had the vital consequence – as the ECJ recognized in its judgment – of making the national courts the principal instrument for the effective application of Community law. Otherwise, enforcement of Community law would have been left almost entirely to the discretion of the European Commission, which could take enforcement action before the ECJ against Member States, but which used that broad discretionary power very hesitantly in the first decades of Community law.

Third, the principle of direct effect led naturally to the recognition of the primacy of Community law. If Community law was to be applied by the national courts, it had to be applied across the Community as a whole. There was therefore no room for the idea that the application of Community law might conflict, in some Member States, with the national law. Community law must necessarily prevail over national law. That was indeed inherent in the very idea of a Community based on the rule of law. The primacy of Community law, resulting both from the inherent logic of the Community system and from the *van Gend en Loos* judgment of 1963, was spelt out in the *Costa v. ENEL* judgment in 1964.[3]

Primacy

In *Costa v. ENEL* the ECJ stressed the unique character of the EEC Treaty:

---

[3] *Costa* v. *ENEL* [1964] ECR 585.

> In contrast with ordinary international treaties, the
> Treaty has created its own legal system which, on entry
> into force of the Treaty, became an integral part of the
> legal systems of the Member States and which their
> courts are bound to apply.

On the special character of the EEC Treaty the ECJ has developed a detailed statement of the primacy of EC law. In the result, EC law, of whatever status, prevails over conflicting national law, of whatever status. EC law prevails, regardless of whether the national law is prior or subsequent to the EC rule. Although the primacy of EC law is nowhere stated in the Treaty, it can properly be regarded as a necessary consequence of a Community based on law, and most commentators have fully accepted that consequence: it will be found, for example, to be accepted in the leading English textbooks on UK public law, constitutional law and administrative law.

Moreover it has been accepted by the highest courts in the United Kingdom, in a striking departure from constitutional orthodoxy. It involves, necessarily and uniquely, a departure from the sovereignty of Parliament.

The UK Act of Parliament providing for membership of the European Communities, the European Communities Act 1972, recognized the primacy of EC law, which at that time had been fully established and recognized. The Act did its best to provide for it.

Yet it seemed legally and constitutionally impossible, under the doctrine of parliamentary sovereignty, to secure the primacy of EC law in relation to a *future* Act of Parliament. Parliamentary sovereignty meant that no Parliament could bind its successor: where there was a conflict between two Acts of Parliament, the later Act prevailed. But the primacy of EC law, introduced by the European Communities Act 1972, required EC law to prevail even over a future Act of Parliament.

The matter was tested in the UK courts in the *Factortame* cases, where the requirements of a 1988 Act of Parliament, the Merchant Shipping Act 1988, were challenged by Spanish ship-owners as being contrary to Community rules on freedom of establishment and non-discrimination. The House of Lords held, as the court of final appeal and after a reference to the ECJ, that the EC rules prevailed over the Act of Parliament.[4]

Where an Act of Parliament is clearly incompatible with EC law, the British court will disapply the provisions of the Act without a reference to the ECJ. This was done by the House of Lords in the *Equal Opportunities* case.[5]

Jurisdiction of the European Court of Justice

The ECJ has taken a broad view of its jurisdiction: what is particularly relevant for our purposes is that it has done so precisely where that was necessary to ensure observance of the rule of law.

Under the original Treaty text, the ECJ could review legally binding acts of the Council and Commission. The Court has interpreted that text in the light of its purpose, which is to be found in the basic Treaty provision setting out the task of the Court: to ensure the observance of the law in the interpretation and application of the Treaty. That purpose, the

[4] *Factortame Ltd* v. *Secretary of State for Transport (No. 2)* [1991] 1 AC 603.
[5] *R* v. *Secretary of State for Transport ex parte Equal Opportunities Commission* [1995] 1 AC 1.

Court held, could not be fulfilled unless it was possible to challenge *all* measures, whatever their nature or form, which are intended to have legal effects.[6]

Moreover, although the Treaty referred to review of acts of the Council and Commission, in the *Les Verts* case the ECJ held, again in order to ensure observance of the law, that it could review measures of the European Parliament.[7]

Equally, although the Treaty provided that actions for judicial review could be brought by a Member State, the Council or the Commission, the ECJ held that it could entertain certain actions brought by the European Parliament. The Parliament could bring a case before the Court 'provided that the action seeks only to safeguard its prerogatives'. 'The absence in the Treaties of any provision giving the Parliament the right to bring an action may constitute a procedural gap . . . [But] it cannot prevail over the fundamental interest in the maintenance and observance of the institutional balance laid down in the Treaties.'[8]

These bold decisions of the ECJ on the scope of judicial review can be justified as being necessary to guarantee the rule of law. As the Court expressed it in *Les Verts*, the Community 'is a Community based on the rule of law, inasmuch as neither its Member States nor its institutions can avoid a review of the question whether the measures adopted by them are in conformity with the basic constitutional charter, the Treaty'.

Here the ECJ uses for the first time a description of the Treaty as the basic constitutional charter of the Community,

[6] See *EC Commission* v. *EC Council* (the *ERTA* case) [1971] ECR 263.

[7] *Parti Ecologiste Les Verts* v. *European Parliament* [1986] ECR 1339.

[8] *European Parliament* v. *EC Council* [1990] ECR I-2041.

invokes the idea of the rule of law and gives an explicit account of what the rule of law requires.

Moreover the bold approach by the ECJ to the scope of its jurisdiction – which has parallels, as we shall see, in the decisions of other leading courts – can find some justification in the rigidity of the constitutional arrangements of the Community, where any amendment of the Treaty is extraordinarily cumbersome, requiring ratification by all the Member States – a process now also involving popular vote by referendum in some States. None the less, despite such difficulties, it proved possible to endorse the ECJ's decisions by amending the Treaty.

The Treaty now provides expressly for actions against the European Parliament. Moreover, Treaty amendment also provided for actions brought by the Parliament: however, the right of the Parliament to bring proceedings was limited – following the exact wording of the ECJ's judgment – to actions brought for the purpose of protecting its prerogatives.

When the European Community was founded (the European Coal and Steel Community in 1952, the European Economic Community in 1958), the ECJ was set up to protect against misuse of the powers of institutions and to ensure respect by Member States for their Treaty obligations. The importance of ensuring observance of the rule of law can be regarded as justifying a broad interpretation of the Court's jurisdiction, sometimes going beyond the text.

There are powerful arguments for this broad approach, which gives effect to what the Treaty intended.

Hence also the need for an evolutionary interpretation of the Treaty. Under the original Treaty, powers were carefully distributed among the institutions, with a system of 'checks and balances'. The 'Assembly', as it was called, initially had no law-making powers and it seemed unnecessary to grant the ECJ powers of judicial review over the Assembly. But as its powers developed, and it was re-styled 'European Parliament', there would have been a serious lacuna, and a rupture of the balance of power, if alone of the political institutions of the Community (Council, Commission, Parliament), its acts had remained immune from judicial review.

Similarly, it later seemed necessary to recognize a limited right of action for the Parliament, to ensure that the powers conferred on it by the Treaty could not be disregarded by the other institutions. Subsequently, as we have seen, these innovations, introduced by bold decisions of the ECJ, were confirmed by being given Treaty expression.

All this is part of what we mean by rule of law. But could it be said that such an approach is *contrary* to the rule of law – with the courts themselves acting unlawfully, contrary to the text?

The ECJ is not alone in taking a broad view of its jurisdiction: other courts, in different contexts, have taken a similar course; and although the contexts are different the approach is similar where what is at stake is the rule of law. Even English courts, which historically have taken a more literal approach to Acts of Parliament, have cut down Acts seeking to exclude all access to the courts, all possibility of judicial review.[9]

---

[9] See, for example, *Anisminic Ltd* v. *Foreign Compensation Commission* [1969] 2 AC 147 in the House of Lords, *per* Lord Wilberforce.

And there are striking examples from other jurisdictions. Sir Michael Kirby's 2003 Hamlyn Lectures cite an example from the Australian High Court. A federal law sought to ban the Communist Party and to attach disabilities to those persons declared by the Executive to be Communists. The Australian High Court declared the law unconstitutional. There were no express provisions in the Constitution to justify that outcome: instead the Chief Justice, Owen Dixon, relied on a broad political and philosophical understanding of the rule of law, which he treated as a fundamental assumption of the Constitution.[10]

But perhaps the outstanding example of bold approaches to constitutional interpretation, and the most historic, is one which we have already considered: the judgment of Chief Justice Marshall establishing the principle of judicial review of legislation under the US Constitution.[11] That too was fundamental to the establishment of the rule of law.

How are such apparent departures from the text to be justified? In part, by an axiom of legal interpretation. The meaning of the text depends on the context. Constitutional provisions must be given a broad interpretation if fundamental constitutional principles – and above all the rule of law – are to be respected. The objections to extensive interpretation, such as the impairment of legal certainty or the denial of legitimate expectations, do not have much force in this context. They hardly apply where the question is, for example, whether the authorities have acted unlawfully and whether the courts

[10] Sir Michael Kirby, *Judicial Activism* The Hamlyn Lectures 2003 (Sweet & Maxwell, 2004), p. 37 n. 152.

[11] *Marbury* v. *Madison* 5 US (1 Cranch) 136 (1803). See chapter 1.

will intervene. The authorities plainly have no legitimate expectation that their unlawful acts will be maintained. If their unlawful acts have given rise to expectations for others, those expectations can be protected as far as possible when the unlawful acts themselves are quashed.

The correct approach to interpretation, therefore, always raises a prior question: what kind of instrument is being interpreted? It is an approach which is widely followed: more often followed, in fact, than it is articulated.

Both the Australian case and the European case mentioned above also illustrate another important theme: the link between the rule of law and democracy.

The connexion is made in the preamble to the European Convention on Human Rights. Although the preamble is not a perfect piece of drafting – the substance of the Convention is far better – it makes a very clear link between the rule of law, human rights and democracy. It refers to the Governments in the following terms:

> '*Reaffirming* their profound belief in those fundamental freedoms which are the foundation of justice and peace in the world and are best maintained on the one hand by an effective political democracy and on the other by a common understanding and observance of the human rights upon which they depend;
>
> '*Being resolved*, as the governments of European countries which are like-minded and have a common heritage of political traditions, ideals, freedom and the rule of law, to take the first steps for the collective enforcement of certain of the rights stated in the Universal Declaration . . .'

These are not just fine words: they are relevant both to the interpretation of the Convention, as was shown in the *Golder* case,[12] and to the continuing debate about the role of the courts in a democracy.

Article 6(1) of the Treaty on European Union makes, in one of the foundational provisions of the European Union, a similar link between democracy, human rights and the rule of law:

> The Union is founded on the principles of liberty, democracy, respect for human rights and fundamental freedoms, and the rule of law, principles which are common to the Member States.

And the same connections between democracy, human rights and the rule of law are made in establishing the qualifications for membership of the European Union, as we shall see below: the first requirement of a candidate country is that it 'has achieved stability of institutions guaranteeing democracy, the rule of law, human rights and respect for and protection of minorities'.

There may be thought to be an inconsistency, even a contradiction, in these statements of fundamental values. How can it be consistent with democratic principles to give often unelected judges (usually, in Europe, judges are unelected) the final word, which may prevail even over laws made by an elected legislature?

But it is not difficult to think of examples where democratic principles might require such a result: for example,

---

[12] See p. 15 above.

if Parliament were to suspend elections, or withhold voting rights from a significant part of the electorate or outlaw a political party.

When else would courts be justified in having the last word? In general, one might say: precisely for the observance of the rule of law (for example, not removing access to the courts); and for the protection of fundamental rights – including the protection of minorities, which may be especially vulnerable in a system of majority rule. Courts will also often, and perhaps necessarily, have the last word in the protection of a federal system – and in similar systems, now increasingly prevalent in Europe, where power or competence is shared between the centre and the component parts of the State, and where a system of independent adjudication is necessary to protect the federal balance.

Perhaps then the rule of law should be understood today as embodying the supremacy of the law, to ensure that the public authorities, including the former 'sovereign', are, where appropriate, themselves subject to the law. This will imply extensive judicial review including limited review of parliamentary legislation, based on a constitution or quasi-constitutional texts; but also based on certain fundamental values, especially fundamental rights.

What are the fundamental values associated with the rule of law?

So far we have concentrated on certain related aspects of the rule of law – access to courts and judicial review. And they are indeed central. But there are other aspects, other values: what are they, and how are they derived?

49

Here European law provides some good solutions, and perhaps also a good technique, namely by drawing on shared fundamental principles, termed 'general principles of law'.

Fundamental principles: general principles of law

A major source of law within the European Union's legal system is to be found in certain fundamental principles, usually referred to as 'general principles of law'; and these principles, as we shall see, have a close resonance with the rule of law. This is not the written law, as laid down by the Treaties and by Community legislation, but principles largely based on the legal values enshrined in the legal systems of the Member States. In many ways this distinction reflects distinctions familiar in English law, such as the distinction between statute law, made by Parliament, and the common law. We shall look briefly at some of these principles; but they suggest immediately a reflection on the character of the Community Treaties. Inevitably the Treaties provide only a skeleton, not a fully fleshed-out legal system. To do that, the ECJ has resorted to general principles which were scarcely, if at all, mentioned, in the Treaties.

They include such principles as:

- The principle of legal certainty.
- The protection of fundamental rights.
- The principle of equality, not merely in specific sectors, but as a principle of general application: we return to this in chapter 5.
- The principle of proportionality.

50

More recently, further principles have been developed, especially in the field of good governance: the principle of good administration; the principle of transparency; and the right of access for the citizen to official documents.

Where and how are these principles derived? Essentially, they are derived from the legal systems of the Member States. The principles are often invoked before the ECJ when cases are referred to it by national courts. In this and other ways, the ECJ has been able to draw on principles embodied in the national systems. The principles may not be recognized to the same extent in all the systems; but they seem to reflect, to a remarkable extent, shared values. Shared values are of course part of what makes up a community; and in these respects, the European Community can be seen to share, at a fundamental level, some common values.

That the fundamental principles are derived from national law is no doubt reassuring for the Member States and their legal communities which follow the development of Community law. These principles are not invented, or drawn out of thin air, or introduced arbitrarily; rather, they are based on well-established practice. Indeed the ECJ's case-law in these fundamental matters has attracted widespread support: not only has it been widely approved, but where it seemed especially important it has been incorporated by the Member States into the Treaties themselves. And these principles, sometimes observed more fully in some States than others, have crossed over, via the Court's case-law, into other national systems, by a process of cross-fertilization, often for the benefit of national law. We shall see later some illustrations of these principles in action.

One more conclusion which is suggested by this very brief overview is in the domain of jurisprudence. The role of principles lends support, at least in this kind of law, to those, like Ronald Dworkin, who have contended that a purely positivist theory of law, as essentially a system of *rules*, does not do justice to law which goes beyond rules, and to the important part played by principles, which are fundamentally different from rules in their scope and effect.

It can also be contended that the values associated with the rule of law have had a practical impact and have played a part in some remarkable achievements of the European Union.

This seems clearly true in relation to the European Union's own market economy. Indeed a free market seems to thrive best where there is a well-functioning legal system. Later we shall see some of the ways in which this works in practice, for example, how the ECJ's case-law has contributed to the development of the European single market.

But it is perhaps even more clear externally.

First, the law plays a vital role in the European Union's economic relations, whether with its main trading partners, or with developing countries or with others.

But more strikingly, the European Union may benefit, in political, diplomatic and even strategic terms, from the fact that it is seen as an entity based on law, and on values associated with the rule of law, rather than as an emergent superpower with all the dangers attendant on that status.

The best proof that the European Union, with its system of values, is seen positively, and has been so seen from the outset, is the powerful role which it has exercised over the past thirty or forty years, and continuing today: perhaps best described as its roles both as a magnet and as a model. A magnet, which has powerfully attracted other European nations to join; a model, in that some of its aims and achievements, its structure and in particular its judicial system, have been imitated in other continents.

We will come back to this in a later chapter.

The rule of law in international law

The rule of law is also recognized as an ideal in international law. The subject is too vast to be covered here, even in outline. But if we focus again on one aspect, namely judicial settlement, we should note again the advance in the judicial settlement of disputes since the Second World War. Before then, international law was widely regarded as exclusively a matter for States, and judicial settlement very much the exception. Rather, the use of force was the norm.

Landmarks in the development of judicial settlement in international law cover very varied fields: they include such unprecedented phenomena as the European Convention on Human Rights of 1950 providing, as we have seen, for a European Court of Human Rights which made it possible, ultimately if not immediately, for an individual to bring a case against a State before an international court.

They include the expansion of the role of the International Court of Justice and a proliferation of other international courts and tribunals.

In the field of international trade, disputes between States are now regularly settled by the revolutionary machinery established by the World Trade Organization (WTO) Agreement of 1994, which also provides for an Appellate Body, in effect an international supreme court, which has in a short time developed an impressive body of case-law.

And more recently an International Criminal Court has been established on a permanent basis.

Of course there are rogue States, and spectacular breakdowns of international law, but these should not be allowed to conceal the huge progress of the rule of law in recent years in world affairs.

But international law is not only a matter for international courts. Of high importance for the rule of law in international affairs is the recognition and acceptance of international law in the internal law of States and domestic legal systems. Here the European Union has taken a leading part, and it is appropriate now to look at the relationship between EC law and international law.

EC law and international law

The European Union provides a good model here. In its case-law, the ECJ recognizes the binding force of the main sources of international law: both of customary law and of treaties concluded by the European Community and by its Member States. Indeed it recognizes the direct effect of treaties in situations where some of the national systems do not.

The ECJ has also treated what is perhaps the most fundamental treaty in Europe, the European Convention on Human Rights, as if it were binding upon the Community, and has followed scrupulously the case-law of the European Court of Human Rights, even though the European Union itself is not a party to the Convention. Indeed, so closely has the ECJ followed the Strasbourg case-law that the Strasbourg Court, in a recent case, considered that it was unnecessary to control or review the ECJ's decision. We turn to these matters below.

It was at one time widely accepted that EC law was somewhat negative in its attitude to international law. This may have been partly true, and partly based on misunderstanding. It could be explained in part by the need, which the ECJ visibly felt, to distance EC law from traditional international law, as it did in the *van Gend en Loos* case in 1963.[13] EC law was described by the ECJ as 'a new legal order', even if it was still, at the time, a new legal order *of international law*; its effects within the Member States were, according to the Court's case-law, very different from those of other treaties; later, the EC Treaty was even, according to the Court, the basic constitutional instrument of the EC.

Similarly, in an early period, the ECJ was regarded as being somewhat negative towards guarantees of human rights based on national law or on the European Convention on Human Rights, apparently concerned that that might threaten the primacy of EC law.

If there was, at one time, some substance in these views of the ECJ, the position is radically different today. Let me take three examples.

---

[13] *Algemene Transport-en Expeditie Onderneming van Gend en Loos NV* v. *Nederlandse Belastingadministratie* [1963] ECR 1.

United Nations Law

I mention as a first example United Nations law: in recent years, the ECJ has had to consider in various situations the meaning and effect of UN Security Council resolutions. This occurred first in relation to UN sanctions following the war in the former Yugoslavia. A series of cases, including the *Bosphorus Airways* case,[14] which I will discuss shortly, shows the ECJ securing the effective implementation of the Security Council resolutions, while taking account of the interests of individuals affected by the sanctions.

Another recent group of cases – some before the Court of First Instance – have been concerned with measures against terrorism, again implementing UN Security Council resolutions. In the *Yusuf*[15] and *Kadi*[16] cases the Court of First Instance accepted the priority of UN law; indeed its judgment contains some striking pronouncements to this effect. I will not comment further, as the cases are being appealed to the ECJ, but the record certainly demonstrates the openness of the European Courts to UN law and general international law.

Treaties concluded by the Community

I take as my second example the approach of the ECJ to treaties concluded by the European Community itself.

[14] *Bosphorus Hava Yollari Turizm Ticaret AS* v. *Minister for Transport, Energy and Communications, Ireland* [1996] ECR I-3953.

[15] *Yusuf* v. *Council* [2005] ECR II-3535.

[16] *Kadi* v. *Council* [2005] ECR II-3649.

As is well known, the ECJ has taken a broad view of the Community's treaty-making power; and if one takes a broad view of what counts as a treaty, the Community has concluded a large number of treaties – reckoned at more than a thousand. The Court has taken a broad view, also, of its jurisdiction to interpret treaties: thus it has held that treaties – even 'mixed' agreements, i.e. those concluded jointly by the Community and its Member States – constitute 'acts of the institutions of the Community' within the meaning of Article 177, later Article 234, of the Treaty, and therefore fall within its jurisdiction under that Article to give preliminary rulings on their interpretation.

The ECJ's case-law on the interpretation of those treaties is now substantial, and is very positive in terms of international law. The Court has proved ready, in contrast to some of the national legal orders in Europe, to recognize the provisions of such treaties as having direct effect wherever their provisions so admit. The result is that the provisions are directly enforceable in the national courts at the instance of individuals seeking to enforce the treaty obligations. In deciding whether there is direct effect, the Court rightly looks both at the nature of the treaty and at the character of the provision in question. Remarkably, however, it is only in one instance that the Court has held that the treaty by its very nature precludes direct effect: that is in the case of the General Agreement on Tariffs and Trade (GATT), first signed in 1947, and its successor, the WTO Agreement of 1994.

The ECJ does not impose, as a condition of direct effect, the requirements often imposed by other legal orders such as reciprocity. Increasingly also, it seems, the Court is going beyond its earlier case-law, where it seemed to stress, when according direct effect to a treaty, a special relationship between the Community and the treaty partner. In recent cases, for example, it has accorded direct effect both to association agreements with European countries and to a treaty embodying a less close relationship, the Partnership and Cooperation Agreement with Russia.[17]

Similarly the language of the Treaty presents less of an obstacle to direct effect than might be supposed. In one case in which I was Advocate General, I found the issue of direct effect a difficult one, although I reached an affirmative conclusion. The ECJ, however, seemed from its affirmative judgment relatively untroubled by the issue.

The ECJ's policy of openness to treaties of this kind and its very positive treatment of them is apparent also from its approach to their interpretation. It is axiomatic that treaties must be interpreted in the light of their aims and purposes, and in the context in which they operate. It follows that agreements with third States cannot necessarily be given the same interpretation as the treaties establishing the Communities themselves. The Court has therefore sometimes been led to interpret, for example, a free trade agreement with a third State differently from the EC Treaty, even though the wording of the provision in question is identical or very similar. The EC Treaty can be given a 'Community' interpretation going further than would be appropriate for an 'ordinary' treaty. All this is entirely consistent with the classic principles of treaty law and treaty interpretation, as set out in the Vienna Convention on the Law of Treaties 1969.

[17] *Simutenkov* v. *Ministerio de Educacion y Cultura* [2005] ECR I-2579.

In recent years, however, the ECJ has tended to extend the 'Community' interpretation, reached in a purely internal Community context, to treaties concluded by the Community with third States. This has been true in particular of provisions prohibiting discrimination on grounds of nationality. Such provisions have been interpreted within the Community context rather extensively, as exemplified by the well-known *Bosman* ruling,[18] perhaps – in some circles – the most often cited of all the Court's judgments. Essentially, the Court held that sporting associations could not exclude nationals of other Member States from membership of sports teams. But that case-law has now been extended to non-EU nationals, first under Association Agreements with third States where the Agreement was intended to forge a particularly close relationship with the Community, and now even under a less intimate 'Partnership and Cooperation Agreement', in the instant case with Russia.[19]

These cases thus provide a good illustration of the openness of the ECJ to international law in the particular shape of treaties concluded by the Community (or jointly by the Community and its Member States), and a readiness to adopt a maximal interpretation of some of their provisions, especially where the critical issue of equal treatment is at stake.

The European Convention on Human Rights

My third and final illustration of the theme of openness to other legal systems is the evolving approach of the ECJ to a system of law based on a treaty to which the Community

---

[18] *URBSF* v. *Bosman* [1995] ECR I-4921.   [19] *Simutenkov*, n. 17 above.

is *not* a party: the European Convention on Human Rights. The Court in recent years has adopted a very positive approach to the Convention. Over the past ten years, in particular, it has regularly cited, and has sought to follow, the case-law of the Strasbourg Court. That is particularly striking when it is remembered that the ECJ does not generally cite the case-law of any other court. Exceptionally, there are occasional references to, for example, a decision of the International Court of Justice; but these are exceptions which seem to serve only to 'prove the rule'.

For practical purposes, it can even be suggested (as I mentioned in my Opinion in the *Bosphorus Airways* case in 1996) that the position is as if the Community were a party to the Convention, and that the Convention can be regarded as part of Community law and can be relied on as such both in the ECJ and in the national courts where Community law is in issue.

The Strasbourg Court in effect accepted this when it came in turn to decide the *Bosphorus* case in 2005.[20] Here the issue was whether the seizure of a Serbian aircraft by the Irish authorities, under UN sanctions against the former Yugoslavia, violated the property rights of an apparently innocent third party, the Turkish company which had chartered the plane. As the sanctions were implemented in the European Union by an EC regulation, the Irish Supreme Court had referred the case to the ECJ, which had found that the Irish authorities had acted lawfully. But the Irish decision could still be, and was, challenged by the airline in Strasbourg.

---

[20] *Bosphorus Hava Yollari Turizm Ve Ticaret Anonim Sirketi* v. *Ireland* [2005] ECHR 45036/98.

There the European Court of Human Rights reached what may be seen as a remarkable decision of a general character. It examined the overall case-law of the ECJ in the field of observance of fundamental rights, and then set out in detail the judgment of the Court (and the Opinion of the Advocate General) in the Luxembourg proceedings in the *Bosphorus* case.[21] On that basis, it held in effect that, given the standard of scrutiny by the ECJ of Community measures for compliance with human rights, where such scrutiny had taken place it was, and would remain, unnecessary for the Strasbourg Court to conduct its own review.

There are, of course, important qualifications in the Strasbourg judgment. Nevertheless, it provides extraordinary testimony on two points: first, the care which the ECJ has taken to accommodate human rights concerns; second, the willingness of the Strasbourg Court, for its part, to recognize the special features of the EU legal order. There could be few better illustrations of my theme in this chapter.

Conclusions

In this chapter we have been concerned with the fundamental values of a legal system itself: values which are sometimes collectively expressed in the notion 'the rule of law'. This notion of the rule of law also conveys the idea that the ultimate source of authority is no longer the sovereign in the shape of a monarch, or even in the shape of a Parliament; but rather

---

[21] *Bosphorus Hava Yollari Turizm Ticaret AS v. Minister for Transport, Energy and Communications, Ireland* [1996] ECR I-3953.

certain values, or certain fundamental principles, which form an inherent part of a well-functioning legal system.

These basic requirements include the idea of the right of access to a court, the right to a fair trial, the availability of effective remedies; and also the idea that all exercise of power is, with the narrowest exceptions, subject to review by the courts. Even in the United Kingdom, where the tradition of parliamentary sovereignty is so strong, there are developments in this direction, and indeed there are now calls from leading politicians for a written constitution. In that constitution, the notion of the rule of law would no doubt play an important part.

It is of interest that a recent Act of Parliament which itself has an intriguing title, the Constitutional Reform Act 2005, contains an express reference to the 'constitutional principle of the rule of law'; indeed Part 1 is entitled 'The rule of law', although its content is perhaps disappointing. Part 1 consists of a single section, section 1, also entitled 'The rule of law', which says:

> This Act does not adversely affect –
> (a) the existing constitutional principle of the rule of law, or
> (b) the Lord Chancellor's existing constitutional role in relation to that principle.

There is, unsurprisingly, no attempt to define what is meant by the rule of law.

To what extent in a future written constitution would the courts have jurisdiction to review legislation for compatibility with the constitution? It seems to me that the rule of law, properly understood in a modern constitutional context, in some respects would and in some respects would not require the courts to exercise that jurisdiction, and that it is not too difficult to work out the answer. But this is not the place to attempt a full response.

The values I have mentioned form part of the heritage of the common law. But their place has been strengthened by the impact of European law: both by the European Convention on Human Rights and by EC law. For example, the right of access to the courts was held by the Strasbourg Court, contrary to the UK's submissions in the *Golder* case,[22] to be guaranteed by the Convention, so that a convicted prisoner who had been refused permission to bring civil proceedings in the English courts was held to have been treated unlawfully.

As for EC law, there are good examples where that has strengthened English law. Perhaps surprisingly, for example, in the area of judicial remedies. English law has been traditionally very strong on remedies: but essentially private law remedies, for example, injunctions. Some of these remedies, such as 'anti-suit injunctions', have caused great problems under European rules on jurisdiction in civil and commercial cases. Others, such as 'freezing injunctions' (formerly 'Mareva injunctions') have been regarded as valuable. Indeed remedies developed by the English courts have sometimes been taken over in EC legislation, for example, the Intellectual Property Remedies Directive,[23] and in the WTO's Agreement on Trade-Related Aspects of Intellectual Property Rights (TRIPs).

[22] See above, p. 15
[23] Directive 2004/48/EC and Regulation 1383/2003/EC relating to the enforcement of intellectual property law.

But in England, remedies in public law have until recently been weak, as was graphically demonstrated by Harry Street in his 1968 Hamlyn Lectures 'Justice in the Welfare State'. Here Dicey's account of the rule of law simply did not work: officials were not in the same state as the private citizen, and the public authorities benefited from substantial privileges – Crown immunities, Crown privilege, royal prerogative, etc. – and from the lack of will on the part of the courts, the Law Commission and the legislature to intervene. What progress there was in recent years may even have led to some complacency, and it was exposure to European law that provoked some necessary reforms.

One example is the availability of injunctions against Ministers of the Crown. The English courts had taken the view that such enforcement remedies were not allowed under English law. In the *Factortame* litigation already referred to,[24] the House of Lords held, after a reference to the ECJ, that an injunction should be granted.

Lord Bridge said that, under the terms of the European Communities Act 1972, it had always been clear that it was the duty of a UK court to override any rule of national law found to be in conflict with any directly enforceable rule of Community law. There was therefore nothing novel in according supremacy to rules of Community law. Thus 'to insist that, in the protection of rights under Community law, national courts must not be inhibited by rules of national law from granting interim relief in appropriate cases is no more than a logical recognition of that supremacy'.

---

[24] See p. 42 above.

Shortly afterwards, the same result was reached by the House of Lords in a purely domestic context, in the leading case of *Re M*.[25] In that case the Home Secretary had failed to comply with a court order that a refugee should not be deported until his application for asylum had been determined. The case had nothing to do with EC law but plainly involved a serious breach of the rule of law. The question was whether the Home Secretary could be liable for contempt of court. The House of Lords held that he could. It can be assumed that EC law had a positive, if indirect, influence on that outcome.

A second example is in remedies by way of damages. English law has traditionally taken a negative view towards the possibility of damages for unlawful acts of the public authorities. The English rules have been much criticized by scholars and indeed by judges. Other European domestic systems go much further in providing for compensation for unlawful action. EC law, for its part, has developed a comprehensive remedy by way of damages against public authorities (both Community and Member State authorities) for breach of their duties. Thus English courts are required to compensate where there is a breach of a Community right, but are still largely precluded from doing so where there is a breach of a domestic right, which may well be no less important. That double standard seems regrettable, and unlikely to be acceptable for very long.

Thus EC law has led the way, for example, in making available injunctions against Ministers of the Crown; and in creating a real, rather than theoretical (although still very

---

[25] [1994] 1 AC 377.

limited) prospect of compensation for unlawful action. These examples, where other domestic European systems also were in advance of English law, show the value of a European standard.

There are now many positive examples of cross-fertilization between English and European law, examples which might indeed have met with the approval of Miss Hamlyn, given her specific interest in Comparative European Jurisprudence.

5

Fundamental values

In this chapter, I continue with the theme of law and values. Here, we are concerned with fundamental ethical values. How does the law, and how do the courts, respond? How are the courts influenced by prevailing social values? How do they react as values change? How far do their decisions, in turn, influence values? What are the proper limits on the role of the courts?

We must inevitably be selective, trying to select those areas which best illustrate the theme. Some of the questions are old, but they can be seen in a new context. And in particular, in a European context.

Religious freedom

I would illustrate the theme with examples from three areas. The first is religious freedom. This is a relatively recent freedom, which emerged after many centuries of religious persecution in Europe. But what is the proper scope, what are the proper limits, of religious freedom? The issues are extremely topical.

And the subject is appropriate for several reasons. First, it illustrates the problem of conflicting values – for example, in the relationship with freedom of expression. In some respects, religious freedom requires freedom of expression, and perhaps reinforces the need for it. In other respects, there may be a conflict between religious freedom and freedom of expression: or at least, respect for religion may be held to impose some limits on freedom of expression.

Second, the subject illustrates particularly well how far these issues can be addressed at European level, and in particular under the European Convention on Human Rights. How far are there truly European values here? And what are the parameters, the proper limits, of supervision of the national authorities by the European Court of Human Rights – supervision, or control, or intervention or (for some) interference?

Third, the topic is especially appropriate to my theme in a further respect: it shows how, where once religion determined the application of law, it is now the law which of necessity seems to determine the scope of religious freedom.

Article 9 of the European Convention on Human Rights sets out in two paragraphs, in the lapidary style characteristic of the Convention, both the essence of religious freedom and its limitations.

By the first paragraph:

> Everyone has the right to freedom of thought, conscience
> and religion; this right includes freedom to change his
> religion or belief and freedom, either alone or in
> community with others and in public or private, to
> manifest his religion or belief, in worship, teaching,
> practice and observance.

By the second paragraph:

> Freedom to manifest one's religion or beliefs shall be
> subject only to such limitations as are prescribed by law

and are necessary in a democratic society in the interests
of public safety, for the protection of public order, health
or morals, or for the protection of the rights and
freedoms of others.

There is no limitation, therefore, on freedom of thought, conscience and religion in itself; but the freedom to *manifest*
one's religion may be subjected to limitations on the grounds
specified.

Clearly the Court has a delicate task in striking that
balance. The Convention, here as elsewhere, requires a choice
to be made between competing values.

In the first case under Article 9 to come before it, the
European Court of Human Rights made some general pronouncements on the place of Article 9 in the Convention system:

> . . . freedom of thought, conscience and religion is one of
> the foundations of a 'democratic society' within the
> meaning of the Convention. It is, in its religious
> dimension, one of the most vital elements that go to make
> up the identity of believers and their conception of life . . .

And the Court added: 'but it is also a precious asset for athe-
ists, agnostics, sceptics and the unconcerned'. The reason?
'The pluralism indissociable from a democratic society, which
has been dearly won over the centuries, depends on it.'[1]

Of interest here in the first place is the link with
democracy: democracy is envisaged, broadly, as requiring tolerance of the diversity of opinions. This is a valuable insight
into the basis of freedom of thought.

---

[1] *Kokkinakis* v. *Greece* (1993) 17 EHRR 397, at para. 31.

But there is also an element of paradox here. One aspect of the paradox is the apparent contradiction between, on the one hand, the possible, and perhaps seductive, claim of religion to a monopoly of the truth and, on the other hand, that freedom of expression which is otherwise regarded as a vital means to attaining the truth.

Another aspect of the paradox is the apparent contradiction with that 'pluralism' which does not figure expressly in the Convention but which is constantly stressed by the Court as inherent in the Convention system.

It would seem clearly incompatible with such pluralism, to take an extreme case, for religion to dominate the political life of a State: there is no place in Europe for a theocratic regime. But there may also be limits on giving undue protection to a particular religion, whether by its position as an established church or otherwise. Conversely, the State does not have an unlimited power to refuse to recognize a particular religious grouping.

Some helpful indications of the Court's approach can be found in a case against Moldova, brought by the Metropolitan Church of Bessarabia. Moldova refused to recognize that Church, yet only religions recognized by the Government could be practised in Moldova.

The Court observed that in principle the right to freedom of religion for the purposes of the Convention excludes assessment by the State of the legitimacy of religious beliefs or the ways in which those beliefs are expressed. State measures favouring a particular leader, or specific organs of a divided religious community or seeking to compel the community or part of it to place itself, against its will, under a single leadership, would also constitute an infringement of the freedom of religion. In democratic societies the State does not need to take measures to ensure that religious communities remain or are brought under a unified leadership.

Similarly, where the exercise of the right to freedom of religion or of one of its aspects is subject under domestic law to a system of prior authorization, involvement in the procedure for granting authorization of a recognized ecclesiastical authority cannot be reconciled with the requirements of paragraph 2 of Article 9.[2]

The Court also considered that, since religious communities traditionally exist in the form of organized structures, Article 9 must be interpreted in the light of Article 11 of the Convention, which safeguards associative life against unjustified State interference. Seen in that perspective, the right of believers to freedom of religion, which includes the right to manifest one's religion in community with others, encompasses the expectation that believers will be allowed to associate freely, without arbitrary State intervention. Indeed, the autonomous existence of religious communities is indispensable for pluralism in a democratic society and is thus an issue at the very heart of the protection which Article 9 affords.

The Court therefore found (somewhat exceptionally) a violation of Article 9 of the Convention.

A further possible contradiction might lie in the contradiction between protecting the 'precious asset' of religion against assault, while respecting freedom of expression, itself

---

[2] *Metropolitan Church of Bessarabia* v. *Moldova* [2001] ECHR 860, at para.117.

no less vital to a 'democratic society'. The right to freedom of expression, protected by the following Article, Article 10, of the Convention, 'constitutes one of the essential foundations of a democratic society, one of the basic conditions for its progress and for the development of every man'.[3]

How far then do religious sensitivities justify restrictions on freedom of expression? This again is a very topical, and very difficult, issue. Moreover it is a subject on which the laws differ significantly in different European States. In England, blasphemy is still an offence: in some other European countries, the prohibition has been abrogated. There is also the issue whether, if the offence of blasphemy is retained, protection can be limited, as historically under English law, to Christianity, or whether it should be extended to other religions. Such a limitation seems increasingly unacceptable in an increasingly multi-faith society.

The Court has hitherto stepped cautiously. In *Wingrove*[4] the British censors had banned a video on the grounds that it appeared to contravene the British blasphemy law: they considered that its public distribution would outrage and insult the feelings of believing Christians. The Court was understandably cautious. On the central issue, whether a system allowing restrictions to be imposed on the propagation of material on the basis that it was blasphemous was in itself incompatible with the Convention, prudence prevailed. The Court considered that there was not yet sufficient common ground in the legal and social orders of the European nations

[3] *Handyside* v. *United Kingdom* (1976) 1 EHRR 737, at para. 48.
[4] *Wingrove* v. *United Kingdom* (1996) 24 EHRR 1.

to support that conclusion. It added that a wider margin of appreciation was generally available where States were regulating freedom of expression in relation to matters liable to offend intimate personal convictions within the sphere of morals or, especially, religion. In those domains the State authorities were, according to the Court, in a better position than an international court to assess what was likely to cause offence to believers in each country.

While the Court's caution is understandable, perhaps even in certain respects commendable, a more robust approach might be preferable. Although the State authorities may be better placed to assess what is likely to cause offence, that may not be the most appropriate criterion for restrictions on freedom of expression. It may be precisely where there is a likelihood of causing offence – as opposed, for example, to inciting violence – that it is most necessary to protect freedom of expression, which causes no other harm, and is generally a force for good.

It is difficult to define the borderline: demands can be made, on grounds of religious sensitivities, which may seem wholly excessive – an example might be the calls to ban the film of the best-selling novel *The da Vinci Code*. The law should not be heavy handed, especially where freedom of expression is involved. After all, those who might be offended by a book or a film have the option of not reading the book or not seeing the film; or if inadvertently they find themselves doing so, they can stop. Prohibition of free expression cannot be based on the reactions or concerns of the most sensitive.

A further question for debate is whether the protection by the State of only one religion is consistent with pluralism. Or can the State give special recognition to a single religion? Is even the existence and recognition of an 'established' church consistent with that ideal? Some Strasbourg cases provide food for thought on these issues. Consider the case of *Serif* v. *Greece*.[5]

The applicant was elected Mufti, or religious leader, of the Muslim community in Thrace, although another Mufti had already been appointed by the State. The applicant was convicted of having usurped the functions of a minister of religion, and of having worn the robes of such a minister, without having the right to do so. Before the Court of Human Rights the Greek Government contended that it was necessary for the authorities to intervene to avoid creating tension between different religious groups in the area.

The Court observed that tension between competing religious groups was an unavoidable consequence of pluralism. The role of the authorities, however, was not to seek to remove the cause of the tension, thereby eliminating pluralism; rather, it was to ensure tolerance between the rival factions. In a democratic society, according to the Court, there was no need for the State to intervene to ensure that religious communities remained or were brought under a unified leadership.

The Court accordingly found that the reaction of the authorities constituted a violation of the Convention.

Another issue under the head of religious freedom is currently causing much concern. How far should the law protect, and how far may it prohibit, the manifestation of religious beliefs, for example, by way of dress or religious symbols?

[5] [1999] ECHR 169.

The issue has arisen in several countries in Europe with the question of the wearing of garments prescribed by religion, such as the Islamic headscarf. It came before the Strasbourg Court in a Turkish case, *Leyla Sahin*.[6] The University of Istanbul decided that students wearing the Islamic headscarf would be refused admission to lectures, courses and tutorials. The Court (Grand Chamber) held in 2006, by sixteen votes to one, that there was no violation of Article 9 of the Convention.

The Court paid particular attention to the situation of Turkey, a predominantly Muslim society but a secular State, with, one might add, a tradition of religious tolerance. The Court observed that the restriction in issue was based in particular on the principle of secularism, which prevented the State from manifesting a preference for a particular religion or belief, and which could entail restrictions on freedom of religion.

That notion of secularism was consistent with the values underpinning the Convention. Indeed, the Court added that upholding that principle could be considered necessary to protect the democratic system in Turkey. The Court, as is its practice in such cases, does not seek to substitute its own assessment for that of the Turkish authorities, satisfying itself with a low level of scrutiny. It found merely that, in the Turkish context, where the values of pluralism, respect for the rights of others and, in particular, equality of men and women before the law were being taught and applied in practice, it was 'understandable' that the authorities should consider it contrary to such values to allow religious attire of the kind in issue to be worn on university premises.

[6] *Sahin* v. *Turkey*, Grand Chamber, 10 November 2005.

Religious freedom: law and values

How do law and values interact? It seems that, not only do values shape law; also, law even helps to shape values. Even within Europe, where values conflict, the balance between conflicting values is struck differently in different societies.

The European Convention on Human Rights, it seems, has a role to play. It is only, in this area, a 'long stop', or a last resort; but it is a valuable last resort. The Court will intervene only exceptionally, which is right, given the variety of religious traditions and the cultural diversity. But, where a State goes too far in regulating or limiting religious freedom, it is valuable to have a European safety mechanism. And conversely, where the Court considers that the State is fully justified in limiting an improper claim to religious freedom, that too may carry an important message.

The subject of religious freedom, and the illustrations from the Strasbourg case-law, suggest a further thought.

The roles of law and religion have in some ways been reversed: religion retains its huge importance for many, even in secular Western societies; but it is no longer, for many, the ultimate arbiter. At one time, and certainly in Europe until well into the nineteenth century, many would naturally have turned to religion for answers to ethical questions and to the most fundamental issues of social policy. Now, for a variety of reasons, law has supplanted religion for giving answers to many of these questions. Religion has sometimes withdrawn from the arena, recognizing that it is no longer its role to answer all questions, and perhaps fearing also that the answers it gives will prove divisive, thus damaging its own cause.

So, rather than religion shaping the content, and the limits, of the law, it is the law which determines the limits of religious freedom; and serves more generally, in resolving conflicts of competing values. It may be thought that law has some advantages, precisely when it comes to balancing competing interests. And perhaps the law and, in particular, the courts have other, systemic advantages? Here I am merely raising some questions and suggesting some tentative answers.

The law does have the advantage that, while reflecting social values, it can also develop, as values evolve, and respond more flexibly. It can even move ahead of social values, and where necessary provoke or promote change. No doubt there is a complex process here, an interaction between law and social values where the causal connections are difficult to discern.

Perhaps the law – and especially the judicial development of the law – has the advantage also that it proceeds pragmatically, by responding to concrete cases and following a problem-solving approach. It starts from certain principles – in this case, laid down by the European Convention on Human Rights – but the working out of these principles is the fruit of their progressive application, developing over time and responding to changing social needs.

As if these suggestions were not already provocative enough, I would suggest also that there are advantages in a European approach:

• We live increasingly in a multi-faith, multi-cultural society: a European approach supplants what might be a one-dimensional view; it allows for a wider perspective.

- It can be more dispassionate, more objective.
- It can bring in experience from other systems.
- It allows for solidarity: a common response may be useful when basic values are threatened. So it can actually reinforce the protection of those values.
- It has the advantage that it can, as the Strasbourg Court has successfully done, treat itself as having the subsidiary role, leaving issues to the domestic courts and limiting its intervention to cases which cross the threshold: it uses a margin of review which allows for differences while preserving the core values.

I hasten to say that there are of course also certain disadvantages in the use of courts, and in the use of European courts. I will turn later to some of those disadvantages.

But perhaps what is most striking is the role that the courts already have, as the arbiter between conflicting values.

Equality: the principle of equal treatment

The general theme of the role of values in the law, and in judicial development of the law, can be well illustrated from another area: the principle of equality, or equal treatment.

And first let me seek to show why it is a good example.

In some ways, equality can be regarded as *the* fundamental value of the law and of justice – both require treating like cases alike. The principle is recognized as a fundamental principle of modern legal systems; whether it takes the form of the principle of equal treatment or the prohibition of discrimination, it is universally recognized.

That does not mean that the principle is applied in the same way. Crucially, its application depends, first, on what situations are to be counted as equal; and, second, (although these two aspects can also be regarded as aspects of the same question) in what circumstances a difference of treatment may be justified.

The principle of equality is also a good example because although it may seem rather a formal requirement, in fact it shows that courts have to grapple with acute value judgments, which have inevitably become increasingly complex, and increasingly controversial.

Indeed, in some areas, the principle has been revolutionary in its implications: literally so, in the example of the French Revolution, and perhaps also in the American Revolution; metaphorically so, in more recent times.

Discrimination on grounds of race

For many years, we may note in passing, the slogan of equality did not inhibit racial discrimination. In the United States, the Supreme Court took a leading part in outlawing that form of discrimination, notably in the domain of education in *Brown* v. *Board of Education*,[7] only in 1954. In that case the Supreme Court reversed its earlier ruling of 1896 in *Plessy* v. *Ferguson*,[8] in which the Court had held, with one dissent, that State-imposed segregation in public facilities was not 'unreasonable' and therefore did not violate the equal

[7] *Brown* v. *Board of Education of Topeka* 347 US 483 (1954).
[8] 163 US 537 (1986).

protection clause of the Fourteenth Amendment to the United States Constitution.

In *Brown*, the Supreme Court reversed itself and held that the clause prohibited racial segregation in education. With a brisk and unexpectedly unanimous opinion running to only ten pages, Chief Justice Warren can be said to have ignited a legal and social revolution in race relations. Warren later disclosed in his memoirs that the opinion was deliberately written in a non-technical style so that it could be understood by laymen and reprinted in the Press.

In Europe, discrimination on grounds of race has had a less spectacular judicial impact, but differential treatment on that ground will be strictly scrutinized.

In the *East African Asians* case,[9] in which the UK Commonwealth Immigrants Act 1968 was challenged under the European Convention on Human Rights as embodying racial discrimination, the European Commission of Human Rights in a preliminary decision declared in 1970 that 'discrimination based on race could . . . of itself amount to degrading treatment within the meaning of Article 3 of the Convention'.

The Commission added that 'it is generally recognized that a special importance should be attached to discrimination based on race, and that publicly to single out a group of persons for differential treatment on the basis of race might . . . constitute a special form of affront to human dignity'.

---

[9] European Commission of Human Rights, decision on admissibility, 10 October 1970; report, 14 December 1973.

Discrimination on grounds of sex

However, the area of equal treatment which is unquestionably the most significant in Europe for examining the role of the courts is the abundant case-law concerned with discrimination on grounds of sex.

Here my examples come mainly from EC law, and they illustrate a combination of both judicial boldness and judicial caution.

First and foremost is the principle of equal pay for men and women, proclaimed in very general terms in the EEC Treaty. Originally it was inserted in the Treaty for essentially economic reasons, rather than in the interest of the abstract principle of equality: the aim was to avoid unfair competition between countries which already practised equal pay and those which did not. But, under the impetus of the European Court of Justices, it took on a life of its own.

First, in a remarkable decision in *Defrenne II* in 1976,[10] the ECJ held that the provision had direct effect, and so was immediately enforceable in the national courts. In subsequent case-law the Court went on to apply the principle in circumstances for which it was very probably not intended: an extreme example being the *Barber* case,[11] where the principle was applied to guarantee equal retirement ages for men and women in private occupational pension schemes: an example which was extreme not of course because the principle was applied in favour of men, but rather because it sits oddly with

[10] *Defrenne* v. *Sabena* [1976] ECR 455.
[11] *Barber* v. *Guardian Royal Exchange Assurance Group* [1990] ECR I-1889.

the fact that different retirement and pensionable ages for men and women were still accepted in the State sector.

Elsewhere the ECJ has proved more cautious in applying the principles of equal pay and equal treatment. The scope of the prohibition of discrimination on grounds of sex has been tested in a variety of contexts. The Court refused, in *Grant* v. *South-West Trains Ltd*,[12] to extend equality to sexual orientation. Thus where an employer offered travel concessions for the spouse of an employee or, under certain conditions, for an unmarried opposite-sex partner, those concessions could not be claimed for a same-sex partner. On the other hand, the Court in *P* v. *S*,[13] urged by the Advocate General to be 'courageous', did apply the principle of equal treatment to the highly exceptional case of transsexuals in the employment context.

Affirmative action

A good example of our general theme is provided by the approach of the ECJ to a key policy area in the implementation of the principle of equal treatment, namely the issue of affirmative action. In relation, for example, to sex equality, to what extent can the authorities justify not merely strictly equal treatment, but the more favourable treatment of the hitherto disadvantaged sex?

The issue is one of general importance which has received special attention, not least from the courts, in the United States.

---

[12] [1998] ECR I-621.   [13] [1996] ECR I-2143.

The ECJ had at first refused, but later accepted under certain conditions, the legitimacy of affirmative action, which is at first sight contrary to the principle of equal treatment, where a justification was advanced that such action was desirable in the interest of the disadvantaged sex. Perhaps here the Court could be seen as in part responding to fierce criticism from pressure groups, or even, as has been suggested, genuflecting to political correctness; but there are powerful arguments for accepting the notion of affirmative action.

The example is helpful as illustrating the value choices which have to be made by the ECJ, and its difficulties in tracing the appropriate line of response. The more so because it is one of the most controversial areas of the Court's case-law, in one of the most sensitive fields.

Article 2(4) of the EC Equal Treatment Directive[14] allows Member States, by way of exception, to take unequal action defined as follows: 'measures to promote equal opportunities for men and women, in particular by removing existing inequalities which affect women's opportunities'. How was this exception to be understood? Two cases illustrate the difficulties.

In *Kalanke* v. *Bremen*[15] the Bremen law in issue provided that female candidates for a job or for promotion were to be given priority over male candidates with the same qualifications in sectors where women were under-represented.

---

[14] Directive 76/207/EEC on the implementation of the principle of equal treatment for men and women as regards access to employment, vocational training and promotion, and working conditions.

[15] *Kalanke v. Freie Hansestadt Bremen* [1995] ECR I-3051.

A man and a woman who were shortlisted for a job in the Bremen Parks Department were considered to have equal qualifications; the woman was appointed because women were under-represented in that department. The unsuccessful applicant, Mr Kalanke, challenged the decision in the German courts and the case was referred to the ECJ.

The Court held that Article 2(4) of the Directive could not authorize a measure such as the Bremen law. Article 2(4) did allow, according to the ECJ, 'national measures relating to access to employment, including promotion, which give a specific advantage to women with a view to improving their ability to compete on the labour market and to pursue a career on an equal footing with men'. But national rules guaranteeing women 'absolute and unconditional priority for appointment or promotion' went beyond the promotion of equal opportunities and fell outside the scope of Article 4(2).

Indeed the ECJ considered that 'in so far as it seeks to achieve equal representation of men and women in all grades and levels within a department, such a system substitutes for equality of opportunity as envisaged in Article 2(4) the result which is only to be arrived at by providing equality of opportunity'. It imposed, in other words, not *equality of opportunity*, but *equality of outcome*.

The ECJ's reasoning seems, on the wording of Article 2(4), absolutely correct – although perhaps not 'politically correct'. The Bremen measure in issue was clearly not a measure for promoting equal opportunities, which was the concern of Article 2(4): instead, it guaranteed a female applicant success where qualifications of male and female applicants were equal.

None the less the judgment understandably proved highly controversial, and was the subject of intense criticism. It was out of line with enlightened trends going further in the direction of affirmative action – including the Community's own evolving policy in this area at that period.

Indeed, shortly after the judgment was delivered, the European Commission issued a statement suggesting that the judgment was limited to measures giving women an absolute and unconditional right to appointment or promotion; it added: 'The Commission therefore takes the view that quota systems which fall short of the degree of rigidity and automaticity provided for by the Bremen law have not been touched by the Court's judgment and are, in consequence, to be regarded as lawful.'

Although the Commission's intervention demonstrates the sensitivity of the issue, the question remained whether this was a correct interpretation of the *Kalanke* judgment. The matter was soon tested in a second case before the ECJ, again a reference from a German court.

In *Marschall*[16] the facts were similar: a man applied for promotion, in this case in the civil service, but an equally qualified woman was appointed on the basis of a rule on affirmative action. But the rule was different. The basic rule was similar in its effect to that in *Kalanke*: it provided that, where there were fewer women than men in the higher-grade posts, women were to be given priority for promotion in the event of equal suitability, competence and professional performance. But there was a proviso: priority for women

---

[16] *Marschall* v. *Land Nordrhein-Westfalen* [1997] ECR I-6363.

was not automatic, and would not apply if reasons specific to an individual (male) candidate tilted the balance in his favour.

The ECJ held, in effect, that because of that difference, this case could be distinguished from *Kalanke*. The measure in issue in *Marschall*, because of the 'saving clause', was permissible under Article 2(4) of the Directive.

Contrary to what some commentators have suggested, there seems to be no indication that the ECJ intended to overrule *Kalanke*: the Court merely distinguishes the two cases. Nevertheless, the later case does cast some doubt on the correctness of the earlier decision.

Although, as Advocate General in *Marschall*, I argued that the two cases could not properly be distinguished, I have much sympathy for the more relaxed approach taken by the ECJ in the later case. Even if it was in part a response to the fierce criticism of *Kalanke*, it does not follow that the later decision was wrong. It is true that the text of Article 2(4) of the Directive counts against the Court's view. But it must be accepted that, whereas normally a derogation from a fundamental right should not be interpreted broadly, here the situation is different. Here it can be argued that a broad interpretation of Article 2(4) does contribute to the achievement of the Directive's underlying aims.

Moreover, if the more relaxed view taken by the ECJ in *Marschall* does depart from the text, it is by no means a characteristic example of 'judicial activism'. Rather the reverse, for the effect of the Court's decision is to enlarge, rather than restrict, the powers of the Member States to conduct and develop their own policies in this sensitive area. Within limits, they remain free to pursue policies of affirmative action.

Subsequently the matter was, unusually, clarified by Treaty amendment. The Amsterdam Treaty introduced in Article 141 (formerly Article 119) of the EC Treaty a new provision expressly providing a broader base for affirmative action. The precise issue considered in the case-law has been overtaken by that amendment. But the cases we have looked at provide one of the best illustrations of the inescapable role of the Court in determining the limits of State and Community action in important areas of social policy, and of the part played in that process by the need to adjudicate where fundamental values conflict.

Moreover, even with the Treaty amendment, it will remain the task of the ECJ to determine its limits; that task will of necessity remain with the Court. The Treaty, like ordinary legislation, can go so far and no further. The detailed contours remain a matter for the Court, and will require value judgments.

Similar considerations apply to other matters touched on above, for example, the treatment of discrimination on grounds of sexual orientation and discrimination against transsexuals.

General considerations on equality

On all these very sensitive issues, the final decision rests with the ECJ: occasionally but very rarely the Member States will agree on Treaty amendment. It is significant that Treaty amendment has been achieved on two particularly sensitive fronts: on sexual orientation and on affirmative action.

We can also see some of the advantages, and some of the difficulties, of a European approach. There is an opportunity for the law sometimes to reflect, and sometimes to develop, common values. The impact of European law in this field has also played a large part in improving (especially) women's rights in the United Kingdom and in some other countries where there were substantial disadvantages for women in (especially) employment. In social and economic terms also, although equal treatment is no longer primarily aimed at avoiding a competitive disadvantage for Member States which already respect it, none the less it is clearly beneficial if it is practised on a Europe-wide basis.

Promotion of equal treatment, not only between men and women but in other sectors as well, can have a positive effect on opinion. Equal treatment in employment matters is surely now accepted as the norm: few would consciously seek today to justify discrimination. That represents in itself a great social advance.

Many employers long resisted equal treatment, and complied only when it proved expensive to resist. But many employers, and other groups in society, would now take as their starting-point not the question of cost, but the question of fairness.

It may be hoped that the same will prove true of more recent issues of discrimination: discrimination on grounds of sexual orientation and discrimination on grounds of disability. Especially in areas such as these, the law can lead opinion, and can influence social attitudes.

In Luxembourg the Government has in recent years run a campaign under the simple slogan: 'All different; all equal.' It is a principle which resonates strongly today.

Yet the principle of equal treatment seems constantly to have new manifestations. I remember Professor Eric Stein of the University of Michigan telling me more than thirty years ago that in the United States, age discrimination was then the latest issue. We have caught up, as of 2006, with our own age discrimination law in the UK, implementing a European Directive. I must say that I find myself taking an increasing interest in age discrimination, for reasons which may be all too apparent.

And after race, sex and age, what next? One suggestion is 'species discrimination': why, after all, discriminate in favour of the human species?

Law and human life

The right to life is, in an obvious sense, the most fundamental right of all.

The right to life and the death penalty

The right to life is the first right protected under the European Convention on Human Rights. Article 2(1) of the Convention states: 'Everyone's right to life shall be protected by law.' It then makes a specific exception for capital punishment; Article 2(1) continues: 'No one shall be deprived of his life intentionally save in the execution of a sentence of a court following his conviction of a crime for which this penalty is provided by law.'

Article 2(2) makes further exceptions:

Deprivation of life shall not be regarded as inflicted in
contravention of this Article when it results from the use
of force which is no more than is absolutely necessary:
(a) in defence of any person from unlawful violence;
(b) in order to effect a lawful arrest or to prevent the
    escape of a person lawfully detained;
(c) in action lawfully taken for the purpose of quelling a
    riot or insurrection.

It is of interest to reflect on the exception made for capital punishment. When the Convention was drawn up, the death sentence was not uncommon. In the United Kingdom it was
abolished for murder only in 1965, and completely abolished
later still. Values in such a field do evolve.

The Sixth Protocol to the Convention, dating back to
1983, abolished the death penalty, with the sole exception of the
penalty imposed in respect of acts committed in time of war or
of imminent threat of war. It has been signed by all member
States of the Council of Europe, and ratified by all but one.

The Thirteenth Protocol to the Convention, signed at
Vilnius in May 2002, abolishes the death penalty completely. It
provides by Article 1:

The death penalty shall be abolished. No one shall be
condemned to such penalty or executed.

By Article 2, no derogation is allowed from those provisions,
even in time of war or other public emergency threatening the
life of the nation. And by Article 3, no reservation of any kind
may be made. The prohibition is absolute. The Thirteenth

Protocol has been ratified by more than thirty member States of the Council of Europe. It is the policy of the Council of Europe to require all new member States to undertake to abolish capital punishment as a condition of their admission to the organization.

The prohibition of the death penalty marks out Europe from systems which in other respects may be comparable, notably the United States. Indeed the cause of global abolition has been vigorously pursued by the European Union. The European Union and all its Member States collectively have regularly urged the United States and other recalcitrant countries to change their practice with regard to the death penalty. There have recently been signs of improvement in the US practice.

Nevertheless in the case of *Soering* the European Court of Human Rights held that the extradition by the United Kingdom of the applicant, Soering, to the United States in circumstances where he risked being exposed to the 'death row' phenomenon would be a breach by the United Kingdom of its obligations under Article 3 of the Convention prohibiting torture and inhuman or degrading treatment or punishment.[17]

But we should also bear in mind that the law in Europe moved ahead of public opinion. If the UK legislation abolishing the death penalty had been put to popular vote in Britain in 1965, it is doubtful if it would have been enacted then. But there is probably more support for its elimination now than there would have been forty years ago. As with the principle of equal treatment and other fundamental value choices, the law

---

[17] *Soering* v. *United Kingdom* (1989) 11 EHRR 439.

can influence values, just as changing values can influence the development of the law. This is a two-way process.

And the process can benefit from European influences. The Convention system has enabled the more progressive attitudes to influence the development of the law, which in turn affects the less progressive. Just as the law can be a step, but not too far, in advance of opinion, so the European standard can be a step, but not too far, in advance of the overall average in Europe.

We should look briefly, with this in mind, at cases where the right to life, and the sanctity of life, have been in issue.

Law and medical ethics

The last example, which I can treat only in outline, concerns profound problems on the borderlines of law and medical ethics in relation to human life.

In the past, it was often said that law was one thing, ethics another; by that I don't mean that law was readily seen by its critics as unethical. Rather, what the law required and what was ethically right were two wholly separate issues. The positivist view, which prevailed in England for centuries, insisted on a rigid theoretical distinction.

The position now is very different: the courts will be anxious to take account of the latest developments in medical science, and will also be concerned that their decisions broadly accord with developments in medical ethics.

I will mention two European examples, one from the ECJ and one from the Strasbourg Court.

The case before the ECJ concerned a newly adopted EC Directive harmonizing the laws of the Member States governing the issue of patents for biotechnological inventions.[18] The Directive was highly controversial: the main thrust of the public debate covered a range of ethical issues, including widespread concerns about the very principle of patenting such inventions, at least in relation to human biotechnology. Some of those concerns were expressed in the notion: 'No patent on human life.'

Concerns were especially great in the Netherlands, and the Netherlands challenged the validity of the Directive before the ECJ on a number of grounds. Ultimately the Court rejected the challenge on all grounds.[19] As Advocate General in the case, I did not escape lightly, having reached in my Opinion the same outcome, that the challenge to the Directive must fail. To my dismay a former student of mine, now an eminent professor and specialist in the field, wrote to me to say that my Opinion was itself a violation of human rights. Fortunately we were subsequently reconciled.

The case raised serious issues, not only in relation to human rights, but also on other ethical issues; on the relationship of the Directive to other international conventions; on the Community's competence under the Treaty to enact the measure; and on other important grounds of challenge.

The Strasbourg case, *Pretty* v. *United Kingdom*,[20] raises in stark, even tragic, form the issue of euthanasia and the

[18] Council Directive 98/44/EC on the legal protection of biotechnological inventions.

[19] *Netherlands* v. *European Parliament* [2001] ECR I-7079.

[20] [2002] 35 EHRR 1.

quality of life. In effect, does the right to life, in Article 2 of the Convention, include also a right to die? The applicant, Diane Pretty, suffered from motor-neurone disease, which was untreatable and resulted in the progressive weakening of her muscles. The Court's judgment describes her plight as follows:

> The disease is now at an advanced stage. She is essentially paralysed from the neck down, has virtually no decipherable speech and is fed through a tube. Her life expectancy is very poor, measurable only in weeks or months. However, her intellect and capacity to make decisions are unimpaired. The final stages of the disease are exceedingly distressing and undignified. As she is frightened and distressed at the suffering and indignity that she will endure if the disease runs its course, she very strongly wishes to be able to control how and when she dies and thereby be spared that suffering and indignity.

Although it is not a crime to commit suicide under English law, the applicant was unable, because of her condition, to end her life without assistance. But it is an offence to assist another to commit suicide. She wished her husband to be able to assist her suicide without risk that he would be prosecuted. The UK authorities had refused to give any assurance to that effect.

The Strasbourg Court was unable to find a violation of Article 2. It pointed out that its case-law had stressed the positive duty of the State to protect human life. It was not possible to interpret the Convention as imposing a negative duty: to read into Article 2, in effect, a right to die, free from interference by the State.

The Court's judgment reflected the prevailing view in most European countries at the time. But this is perhaps an area in which one might see developments in opinion, and in the case-law, in the future. It is now forty-five years since, under the Suicide Act 1961, suicide ceased to be an offence under UK law.

I cannot do better here than cite Stephen Sedley:[21]

> From a theologically-determined situation in which suicide was, absurdly, a crime, we have now come to accept that the right to life, as an aspect of personal autonomy, includes a right to die. But it is a right which is heavily constrained. It permits you at least to take your own life without becoming a criminal in the process. It enables you, if you are in command of your faculties, to refuse treatment both now and – subject to sensible statutory conditions – prospectively. But is does not allow anyone to help you die. Nor does it, at present, allow you prospectively to request termination by making a living will.
>
> The case for changing these aspects of the law in favour of greater personal autonomy is heavily contested. I am not going to try to grapple with the arguments advanced from positions of faith which have rarely had a problem about endorsing hanging or war, but which here seek to deny people the power to assure for themselves the quietus that the virtuous have always been prepared to hand out to the wicked. I do acknowledge the secular concern that it may be principally women who choose to die rather than be a burden to their families, replicating life's inequalities in death. I acknowledge also the legitimate concern that relatives who stand to benefit by a patient's death will try

---

[21] Holdsworth lecture 2005, University of Birmingham.

to accelerate it: where there's a will, there's a relative, as the saying is. Yet, acknowledging all this, it remains increasingly hard to deny to sane people facing a drawn-out and degrading death – not necessarily a painful one – the right to say they've had enough. If human dignity and autonomy are among the core values which shape the human rights agenda, the case for a right to die with dignity is a powerful one. If so, a need for help in the process is often an inescapable part of the right.

Conclusions

The topics chosen in this chapter are inevitably selective, but perhaps not unrepresentative. Many other examples could have been chosen. They would, I think, serve also to demonstrate, if in different ways, the role of the courts, and the impact of the European Courts, in determining the scope of the fundamental rights laid down by law, and in both reflecting and shaping our values.

6

Courts and free markets

Here we turn to the European Community, and to economic issues: to the role of the European Court of Justice (ECJ). We shall consider the role of the courts in fashioning a free economy, and in determining its limits.

The approach of courts traditionally favours, here as elsewhere, the freedom of the individual: here, the freedom of the trader. The English courts historically regarded a restraint of trade as contrary to public policy. But what are the limits on that approach? What happens, especially, when free trade conflicts with other values?

The EC internal market

My first example is from the internal market, and serves to illustrate the role of the ECJ. It should be stressed at the outset that the internal market is about far more than free trade in goods and services, hugely important though they are; it is also about the free movement of persons, individual rights and the development of fundamental principles in that context, in particular the principle of equal treatment. Article 14 of the EC Treaty refers to the internal market as comprising 'an area without internal frontiers, in which the free movement of goods, persons, services and capital is ensured'. This sector of the law has seen remarkable developments. But I will start with free trade in goods, the first substantive topic in the EC Treaty.

Here, the need for a strong court to counter the protectionist urges of governments can be abundantly illustrated from the ECJ's case-law, which has consistently championed the effective enforcement of the Treaty provisions on the free movement of goods in particular.

Indeed the topic provides a good overview of the development of Community case-law. The *van Gend en Loos* judgment in 1963, perhaps the single most important judgment in the history of the Community, establishing the direct effect of the Treaty, was concerned with a restriction on imports.[1] The *Dassonville* judgment in 1974 laid down an extraordinarily wide formula, treating the Treaty provision as covering, and in principle prohibiting, 'all trading rules . . . which are capable of hindering, directly or indirectly, actually or potentially, intra-Community trade'.[2]

In the same spirit, the exceptions provided by the Treaty, on grounds of public policy, public health, etc., have been strictly construed by the ECJ, which has been regularly robust in its rejection of protectionist pretexts advanced by governments.

Public health arguments have been favourites with governments. The ECJ has rightly held that human health and life rank first among the interests protected by Article 30 and that, in the absence of Community legislation in the matter, it is in principle for the Member States to decide on the degree to which they wish to protect human health and life and how that degree of protection is to be achieved.

---

[1] *Algemene Transport-en Expeditie Onderneming van Gend en Loos NV* v. *Nederlandse Belastingadministratie* [1963] ECR 1; see p. 39 above.
[2] *Procureur du Roi* v. *Dassonville* [1974] ECR 837.

But that does not give the Member States a free hand: measures taken to protect public health must not go beyond what is necessary to achieve that aim.

There are legion examples in the case-law. France tried to justify taxing whisky, which happens to be Scottish, more heavily than brandy, which happens to be French, on the ground that whisky is more harmful: the ingenious argument was that whisky is often drunk before meals, and so on an empty stomach. The defence failed.

Germany tried to justify its beer purity law, which effectively excluded all imported beer, on the ground of the danger of ingesting additives, given the very large quantities of beer consumed by German drinkers, in particular those consuming more than 1,000 litres a year. Those arguments did not prevail.

In the famous judgment in *Cassis de Dijon* in 1979 a similar issue arose, but the ruling had far-reaching repercussions for the law on the free movement of goods.[3]

'Cassis de Dijon' is a blackcurrant fruit liqueur made in France. It could not be imported into Germany because its alcoholic strength was too low to satisfy the requirements of German law.

While one can readily understand that a maximum alcoholic strength might be considered necessary on grounds of public health, it may at first sight seem more difficult to justify a minimum requirement on that ground. Germany's public health argument was that the requirement for fruit liqueurs to have a

---

[3] *Rewe-Zentral AG v. Bundesmonopolverwaltung für Branntwein* (the *Cassis de Dijon* case) [1979] ECR 649.

minimum alcohol content of 25 per cent prevented a proliferation of low-alcohol drinks on the market, which might more readily lead to tolerance towards alcohol than stronger drinks.

The ECJ again was not persuaded. However, it took the opportunity to re-examine the scope of the Treaty provisions. And it introduced a key notion for the internal market: that goods which have been lawfully produced and marketed in one Member State can in principle be sold in another Member State without further restriction or control.

The result is to replace dual regulation of a product – that is, regulation by both the home State and the importing State – with single regulation, by the home State: regulation which, under the principle of mutual recognition, the importing State is required to respect.

Thus the judgment has a powerful deregulatory effect. First, it cuts out the dead wood of centuries of regulatory tradition in all Member States. And it has probably made unnecessary a great deal of harmonization by Community legislation of product requirements and the like. At the same time, by a well-judged balancing act, the judgment accepts the need for restrictions on trade which are genuinely justified by requirements in the public interest: the ECJ refers 'in particular' (so the list is not closed) to the following:

- fiscal supervision;
- public health;
- the fairness of commercial transactions; and
- the defence of the consumer.

Subsequently, however, the ECJ drew back from its very broad prohibition of restrictions on imports. It considered that a broad prohibition might go too far in precluding national regulation. In particular, it could be improperly exploited to challenge national measures which had a rather limited effect on imports and were not within the intended ambit of the Treaty.

The ECJ accordingly devised a new exception. In *Keck*[4] there was a challenge to a national measure limiting sales at a loss. That, it was contended, could restrict imports from other Member States. That was a step too far. The Court introduced the idea that, contrary to previous case-law (unspecified), the Treaty prohibition did not apply to 'certain selling arrangements' (also unspecified) provided that such arrangements were not discriminatory.

Apart from the lack of precision in the judgment, the new rule seemed to some, including me, unsatisfactory: on a proper analysis, it was difficult to justify a requirement of discrimination; and I would have preferred, as I suggested in my Opinion in the *Leclerc-Siplec* case,[5] a market-related criterion, specifically, whether the measure was liable substantially to restrict access to the market.

That criterion was not accepted in the *Leclerc-Siplec* judgment itself; but some commentators consider that the ECJ has since moved away from the *Keck* formula and has moved in the direction of the market access criterion.

What is not disputed is that the ECJ has generally, and rightly, been rigorous in its scrutiny of Member State defences. In examining them, it has generally applied stringently, in particular, the key principles of non-discrimination

---

[4] *Keck and Mithouard* [1993] ECR I-6097.

[5] *Société d'Importation Edouard Leclerc-Siplec* v. *TF1 Publicité SA* [1995] ECR I-179.

and proportionality. It has had the inescapable task of balancing the interests of free trade against other public interests and values.

The ECJ has also, as we shall see, applied in this field other fundamental principles of due process and fairness, recognizing in this way the fundamental values of the legal systems of the Member States.

The internal market and the rule of law

Moreover there is a two-way process apparent here: the ECJ, in its case-law on the internal market, has required that similar principles of judicial review should be applied by the national courts; and that those courts should have jurisdiction themselves to review where necessary the decisions of national authorities affecting the exercise of Community law rights. Let me summarize, in outline only, what the principles developed by the Court in this context include:

- the individual must have effective access to his or her national courts to claim Community rights which have direct effect;
- he or she must be able to challenge before his or her national courts the decisions of national authorities affecting his or her Community rights – those decisions must therefore be sufficiently supported by reasoning to enable the national courts to review them;
- the national courts must review such decisions for compliance with the principle of non-discrimination; thus, for example, national law must treat Community rights no less favourably than rights protected by national law;

- the national courts must, when reviewing decisions of national authorities affecting Community rights, apply the principle of proportionality. This is not the place for a full discussion of this principle. It must suffice to make, very briefly, three points.

First, the principle of proportionality requires, among other things, that the authorities do not impose on the individual a burden which is disproportionate to the aim of the measure. As it is often put, the questions to be considered include whether the measure was suitable or appropriate to achieve the desired aim; and whether it was necessary to achieve that aim, or whether a less burdensome measure would have been sufficient.

Second, the principle requires closer scrutiny than the test traditionally applied under English law, namely the so-called 'Wednesbury' test, named after the *Wednesbury* case.[6] That test imposed a low standard of review; it was even stated in that case that to be unlawful, the measure must be 'so absurd that no sensible person could ever dream that it lay within the powers of the authority'.[7]

Third, the principle of proportionality, as well as imposing a higher standard on the authorities, may also require the courts to balance the competing interests: an exercise which was not required under the traditional English-law approach.

- The national courts must provide effective remedies for the enforcement of Community rights.

---

[6] *Associated Provincial Picture Houses Ltd* v. *Wednesbury Corpn* [1948] 1 KB 223.   [7] *Ibid.* at p. 229, *per* Lord Greene MR.

This excursus has I hope shown the need for a single court, and indeed a robust court, to police the single market. But such a court must not be too single-minded, or even too single-market minded. It is interesting to see that in recent cases the ECJ seems more willing to accept some justifications for restrictions on trade, for example, where the State invokes considerations of fundamental rights, as in the *Schmidberger* and *Omega* cases mentioned below. Indeed here the Court's language, in allowing States a certain margin of appreciation, reflects the less exacting scrutiny, and even the language, of the Strasbourg Court.

That approach seems appropriate, or even necessary, since it is essential that the Strasbourg and Luxembourg Courts should be in harmony in their handling of the relationship between EC law and the European Convention on Human Rights.

Free trade and human rights

In recent years, the ECJ has tackled cases where there appeared to be a direct clash between the fundamental economic freedoms of the EC Treaty and fundamental human rights of the kind protected by the European Convention on Human Rights.

A notable example, perhaps the first case in which the issue was explicitly presented in this way, is the *Schmidberger* case.[8]

---

[8] *Eugen Schmidberger, Internationale Transporte und Planzüge* v. *Austria* [2003] ECR I-5659.

The Austrian authorities allowed an environmental group to organize a demonstration on the Brenner motorway, one of the main trade routes between northern Europe and Italy; the result was that the motorway was completely closed to traffic for almost thirty hours. Schmidberger, an international transport company, brought an action for damages in the Austrian courts against the Republic of Austria. It contended that the effects of the Austrian authorities' conduct in allowing the closure of the motorway infringed the EC Treaty provisions on the free movement of goods between Member States. The Austrian authorities defended their conduct on grounds of human rights: assessment of the interests involved should lean in favour of the freedom of expression and freedom of assembly which were fundamental rights, inviolable in a democratic society.

We may note in passing that, although the demonstration was part of an environmental campaign, the conflict here was not between free trade and the environment, but rather between free trade and the fundamental freedoms of expression and assembly: from that point of view, the subject of the demonstration was not relevant to the issue or to the outcome.

The reference of the case by the Austrian court to the ECJ required the latter to undertake a balancing of the interests involved, which it did very explicitly:[9]

> [T]he interests involved must be weighed having regard to all the circumstances of the case in order to determine whether a fair balance was struck between those interests.

[9] *Ibid.* at para. 81.

The language of 'a fair balance' reflects the language of the European Court of Human Rights; but it suggests a more relaxed scrutiny than the ECJ had customarily applied to restrictions on trade. The Court continued, moreover, by accepting, again in Strasbourg-style language, that the national authorities 'enjoy a wide margin of discretion in that regard'.[10]

Nevertheless, the ECJ said, it was necessary to determine whether the restrictions placed upon intra-Community trade were proportionate in the light of their aim, namely the protection of fundamental rights. Having examined the various factors, the Court reached the conclusion – once again referring to 'the wide discretion which must be accorded to them in the matter' – that the authorities 'were reasonably entitled' to consider that the aim of the demonstration could not be achieved by measures less restrictive of intra-Community trade.[11]

In this case the ECJ seemed willing to take a more relaxed line than its previous case-law might have suggested. Various explanations might be advanced, but three points might be mentioned.

First, the ECJ has become more sensitive – as indeed we have already seen – to human rights concerns. Indeed its modern stance is diametrically opposed to its earliest case-law on the subject, in which it rejected any attempt to invoke arguments based on fundamental rights – although that approach prevailed only in the very early years.

This evolution may suggest a further thought: that with the internal market in goods now largely achieved, a more

---

[10] *Ibid.* at para. 82.   [11] *Ibid.* at para. 93.

relaxed view can be taken than was appropriate when the barriers were still in place.

Finally, although the measure in issue here was a national, rather than a Community, measure, and might therefore attract more strict standards of review – justifiably, since national measures are more likely to obstruct the single market – the present case, in contrast to some of the cases we considered earlier, was clearly not one in which there was any protectionist intent or effect.

A second example, perhaps even more striking, is the *Omega Spielhallen* case.[12]

Here the German authorities had banned a game played in a laserdrome operated by the applicant company, which involved the simulated killing of humans using laser guns. The company, Omega, challenged the ban as contrary to the freedom to provide services, since the equipment and technology were supplied by a British company.

The case again raised the issue of a conflict between fundamental economic freedoms under the EC Treaty and fundamental human rights, since the German courts upheld the ban on the ground that the commercial exploitation of a game involving simulated homicide was an affront to human dignity protected by the German Basic Law.

On a reference from the German court, the ECJ accepted that the restrictions on the freedom to provide services satisfied the principle of proportionality: they did not go beyond what was necessary to protect the values in question.

[12] *Omega Spielhallen – und Automatenaufstellungs – GmbH* v.
Oberburgermeisterin der Bundesstadt Bonn [2004] ECR I-9609.

Moreover the Court expressly accepted – and here the ruling perhaps goes further than the previous case-law – that the outcome did not depend upon all Member States having a shared conception of the way in which fundamental rights are to be protected. The Court here recognizes the possibility – or even perhaps the merit – of value diversity.

Other values

The European model, as it might be called, is a middle of the road system which balances the free market against other values. It is a balanced compromise, accommodating both a market economy and a developed welfare State. This is, broadly speaking, a balance long accepted in mainland Europe by the main political parties, sometimes categorized as social democrats and Christian democrats, although with differences of emphasis. Formerly this European model could be contrasted with more extreme models: the socialist model of the former Soviet Union and its satellites; it can still be contrasted with the 'hire and fire' model of the United States.

The balance is reflected in the system of the EC Treaty. For example, the Treaty allows for different systems of 'property ownership'. This is understood as allowing for nationalized industries and State ownership of the means of production. The language now seems old-fashioned, and today privatization has largely prevailed, for pragmatic reasons as well as ideological reasons: State ownership and State control in many (not all) sectors have failed. Indeed this may be one of the underlying causes of the fall of the Berlin Wall. Today the premise of the internal market, as we shall see, is a free economy.

Indeed the State in Europe is now increasingly choosing to distance itself from the control of economic levers: it chooses to guarantee the independence of central banks, and with that to renounce a core instrument of policy, the power to set central interest rates. Indeed it seeks to protect from political control – or interference – key instruments of economic policy.

Generally, the more successful economies in Europe have moved away from State control to a more liberal system. This has become part of the political consensus, no longer contested on party political or ideological grounds; and not least in the United Kingdom.

That new liberal economic order was anticipated by the EEC Treaty. It generally sought to substitute market forces, and the forces of competition, for the role of the State as the regulator of the economy. Article 4(1) of the Treaty, as amended, now refers to economic policies 'conducted in accordance with the principle of an open market economy with free competition'.

Competition

Let me turn briefly to the subject of competition.

While the EC Treaty is neutral in some respects, it is strong on enforcing competition.

Rules applying to 'undertakings'

The EC Treaty contains a clear and succinct chapter on competition. First come the 'Rules applying to undertakings'

(Articles 81 to 86). They have survived essentially unchanged for fifty years.

The main change was introduced recently, and without the need to amend the Treaty. In 2004 the European Commission effectively renounced its role as the principal enforcement agency of the EC competition policy – virtually the only area of EC action where the Commission has that role. A Council regulation,[13] adopted on the proposal of the Commission, transferred much of that responsibility to the national agencies and national courts.

This was a bold application of the principle of sub-sidiarity. It provides little support for the perception of the Commission as a body constantly seeking to extend its powers. It remains to be seen whether the national authorities will be up to the task of enforcing the competition policy as effectively as the Commission has done.

Difficulties may arise in particular where there are competing values: again, competition policy may conflict, in particular areas, with environmental concerns. With the assistance of the Commission, where required, the national authorities should be able to maintain the effectiveness of the EC competition rules.

The effectiveness of EC competition policy can be contrasted with earlier UK approaches. The UK system was formalistic, toothless and out of keeping with the newer economic thinking, in the United Kingdom as well as in Europe.

[13] Regulation 1/2003/EC of 16 December 2002 on the implementation of the rules on competition laid down in Articles 81 and 82 of the Treaty, OJ 2003 L 1, p. 1.

In the European Union, competition and market forces have largely, although by no means completely, replaced the State in determining the direction of the economy. Competition itself has to be protected: against the State, against public undertakings and against undertakings which have a dominant position in the market in question.

The EC Treaty provides a set of clear, cogent and relatively straightforward principles of law which have been remarkably effective and successful in their operation. Their effectiveness is illustrated by the fact that many Member States, including the United Kingdom, have voluntarily copied the EC Treaty rules on competition for the purposes of their internal law – a remarkable example of spontaneous harmonization of the law in Europe.

And this process of harmonization is not confined to Europe. Apparently, at the last count, 110 countries have a body of competition law. Many of those national systems are directly based on the EC rules. That reflects well on the perceived merit of the EC system – although it might partly be due to the fact that many of those countries seem wisely to have called in the same expert to advise them on competition policy, Professor Richard Whish of King's College London.

State subsidy and public services

Other difficult borderline issues in the field of competition arise in relation to subsidies granted by the State. It is essential in a common market that States should be precluded from propping up their own favoured lame industries: one State's subsidy, it has rightly been said, is another State's unemployment. It would be contrary to the very idea of fair competition and the 'level playing-field'.

The EC Treaty accordingly contains provisions on 'Aids granted by States' (Articles 87 to 89). State subsidies are strictly prohibited, subject to limited exceptions, as part of the competition policy of the Treaty.

But again, where is the line to be drawn? It is necessary to take account of public services, serving vital public interests and attracting legitimate support from public funds. The Treaty now contains an Article, Article 16, explicitly recognizing 'the place occupied by services of general economic interest in the shared values of the Union'. Article 16 also recognizes the role of these services 'in promoting social . . . cohesion'.

Where then does State financing escape the prohibition of State aid, and amount to legitimate financing of public services? Again, this seems, perhaps necessarily, a task for the courts. The topic illustrates well the role of the ECJ. There has been intense public debate in recent years, and political debate at the highest level, at European summits. The issue came to a crux in the European Court. There was a series of cases, raising the issue in rather different forms. Differing views were expressed by different Advocates General, and there were initially some rather inconsistent decisions by the Court. The ongoing debate proved constructive. Finally, in the *Altmark* case, the ECJ helped to construct a carefully balanced resolution of the issue.[14]

---

[14] *Altmark Trans GmbH* v. *Nahverkehrsgesellschaft Altmark GmbH* [2003] ECR I-7747.

Environment

Perhaps the best-known example in international thinking on trade today is the conflict between free trade and protection of the environment. It has, quite rightly, captured the public imagination: no less than the future of our planet, and of human life, is at stake here.

It should not, it is true, be assumed that international trade and protection of the environment necessarily conflict. On the contrary they may be seen as complementary values:[15]

> Environment and trade policies should be mutually supportive. An open multilateral trading system makes possible a more efficient allocation and use of resources and thereby contributes to an increase in production and incomes and to lessening demands on the environment. It thus provides additional resources needed for economic growth . . . and improved environmental protection. A sound environment, on the other hand, provides the ecological and other resources needed to sustain growth and underpin continuing expansion of trade.

This presents a rather rose-tinted view, but is a useful corrective to the contrary position. In practice the demands of trade and the environment will often conflict. Legislation is not usually the answer. Many of the issues have had to be resolved by the courts. They decide, in effect, when environment trumps free trade.

Moreover, it is difficult where decisions are taken unilaterally by national courts. There are advantages in

---

[15] Agenda 21, adopted at the UN Conference on Environment and Development in 1992, 31 *International Legal Materials* 881.

multilateral decision-making, although of course some problems too.

It is instructive to look at experience first on the EU level, and the approach of the ECJ; then at the world level, in the World Trade Organization and its dispute settlement mechanism.

In the European Union, the ECJ has acted boldly in the interest of the environment. It even anticipated, in that interest, the subsequent amendment of the EC Treaty, which originally contained no provisions specifically dealing with the environment. There was no basis in the original Treaty for environmental measures. Instead these were adopted by the Community legislature on the basis of the 'residual' Treaty Article, Article 235.

That Article, contained in the 'General and final provisions' of the Treaty, stated that, if action by the Community should prove necessary to attain one of the Community's objectives, and the Treaty had not provided the necessary powers, the Council should, following the prescribed procedure, take the necessary measures.

Article 235 was thus of limited scope, and it required unanimity among the Member States for action to be taken. Nevertheless, on the basis of that Article, there was already a substantial legislative package in place before the Treaty was amended in 1987 by the 'Single European Act' to provide, among many other things, for a specific Treaty basis for environmental measures. (The Act, after thirty years, made the first significant substantive amendments of the Treaty and included a Title on the environment, providing for the first time a specific Treaty basis for environmental legislation.)

It was perhaps the existence of this somewhat premature package of environmental legislation which inspired the ECJ to anticipate the Treaty amendment and to declare, as early as 1985 in the *ADBHU* case, that the protection of the environment was 'one of the Community's essential objectives' when there was nothing at all in the Treaty to support that proclamation.[16]

But the case highlighted another lacuna in the Treaty. Under the Treaty as it then stood, and even under the Treaty today, there is no provision allowing for restrictions on trade to be justified by environmental considerations. The interests which could justify such restrictions are today (under Article 30), as they were in the beginning (under the corresponding Article 36):

- public morality, public policy or public security;
- the protection of health and life of humans, animals or plants;
- the protection of national treasures possessing artistic, historic or archaeological value; and
- the protection of industrial and commercial property.

Protection of the environment is conspicuous by its absence. The interests listed were taken over, when the original EEC Treaty was drafted fifty years ago, from the standard clauses in international trade agreements. The environment was not at that time a major concern.

It is surprising, however, that the opportunity was not taken to amend the Treaty on this score, even when

[16] *Procureur de la République* v. *Association de défense des brûleurs d'huiles usagées* [1985] ECR 531.

environmental concerns were at the forefront of attention. As well as the introduction of an environmental measure in the Single European Act, we may note the prominent new Article 6, introduced by the Treaty of Amsterdam:

> Environmental protection requirements must be integrated into the definition and implementation of . . . Community policies and activities . . .

But according to the text of the Treaty, restrictions on trade, even today, cannot be justified on environmental grounds.

The problem was left to the ECJ, and resolved in the *ADBHU* case.

That case raised directly the issue of conflict between the free movement of goods and the protection of the environment. At issue was a Community measure regulating the disposal of waste oils, Directive 75/439/EEC. The national court asked the ECJ, very pertinently, whether the Directive was compatible with the principles of free trade, free movement of goods, and freedom of competition established by the EEC Treaty.

The ECJ answered that the principles of free movement of goods and freedom of competition, together with freedom of trade as a fundamental right, are not 'to be viewed in absolute terms but are subject to certain limits justified by the objectives of general interest pursued by the Community'.

As to those objectives, the ECJ went so far as to state explicitly, as we have seen, that the protection of the environment was one of the Community's essential objectives: the implication was that environmental interests would carry great weight in the balancing exercise.

In the result, the ECJ held that the measure respected the principles of proportionality and non-discrimination, and was therefore not contrary to the free-trade principles underpinning the Treaty.

In issue in that case was the validity of a *Community* environmental measure, which the ECJ upheld. But the Court's concern for the environment is demonstrated even more clearly in its approach to *Member States'* environmental measures, where these are challenged as contrary to the free movement of goods.

While the ECJ has generally, as we have seen, scrutinized rigorously many of the defences advanced in an attempt to justify restrictions on trade in goods, it has proved remarkably tolerant of environmental justifications. Instead of applying strictly the criteria of non-discrimination and proportionality, the Court has appeared to be more ready to accept environmental arguments; and the Court has sometimes not even answered the charge of discrimination, or has at times answered it unconvincingly.

Many observers would applaud the results – the outcome – of a very substantial and remarkably consistent body of case-law[17] even if they have reservations about the detail of the ECJ's reasoning. It might even be taken as a striking demonstration of the need for an evolutionary interpretation of, at least, constitution-style instruments such as the EC Treaty.

But the lessons I would draw from it for my present purposes are of a different order.

---

[17] See my article on 'The Role of the European Court of Justice in the Protection of the Environment' 18 *Journal of Environmental Law* (2006), at p. 185.

First, it shows very clearly that a court entrusted with giving effect to provisions on free trade cannot escape the duty of balancing that goal against other values.

Second, it must take a position on those other values and their place in the scales.

Third, environmental matters cannot be hived off and considered separately: they must be part of the equation. That, incidentally, demonstrates in my view that there is no merit in the idea of a separate environmental court for issues of this kind. In the vital context of the conflict between free trade and the environment, that idea seems untenable.

Similar considerations apply at the world level, in the World Trade Organization (WTO) dispute settlement procedures, when it resolves, on the international level, disputes between States over free trade. Of interest is the reference in the preamble to the WTO Agreement, which acknowledges that expansion of production and trade must allow for 'the optimal use of the world's resources in accordance with the objective of sustainable development, seeking both to protect and preserve the environment . . .'

Here again the WTO panels, at first instance, and the WTO Appellate Body, on appeal, have inevitably been faced with similar kinds of conflicts between trade and the environment. The shrimp-turtle case and the tuna-dolphin case are among the most famous.[18]

> After a difficult start, the WTO has laid a foundation for
> reconciling actual and potential conflicts between

[18] See Mitsuo Matsushita *et al.*, *The World Trade Organization: Law, Practice and Policy* (Oxford University Press, Oxford, 2003), chapter 20.

international trade and protection of the environment. The new accommodation that has occurred since 1995 is almost wholly the work of the Appellate Body.[19]

It is true that the Appellate Body has been more cautious than the ECJ. It has adopted a more strict, a more literal approach to its founding treaty, the WTO Agreement (or General Agreement on Tariffs and Trade (GATT) 1994). But that is an appropriate response for a world body, and for a rather new tribunal concerned to gain the confidence of well over a hundred members. Nevertheless the balancing exercise is similar in principle to that conducted by the ECJ.

Again it seems clear that the idea, sometimes floated, of a separate environmental body to take a position on these issues at international level is a non-starter. The protection of the environment has to be integrated with the settlement of disputes concerning free trade. That process does not preclude full recognition of the significance of environmental interests.

Free markets and wider freedoms

In addressing courts and free markets, I have focused on the role of the ECJ and in particular on market freedoms. But there may also be connections with other freedoms.

Free markets may generate wider political freedoms; there are links with democracy and fundamental rights.

It is of course very difficult to trace direct causal connections here, but there are many indications which seem to point in this direction. In central and eastern Europe, the first

[19] *Ibid.* p. 829.

signs of a liberalization of the economy emerged in the 1980s, before the political dam burst. Those events may not have been unrelated. The progressive enlargement of the European Union over the past thirty years, one of the most remarkable political events of our age, has not only been about the extension of the single market to former subject States. As we have seen, and will see in more detail in the next chapter, it has also been about the extension of democracy and the rule of law.

Further afield, outside Europe the pattern is far less clear, although it may not be entirely coincidental that the most successful trading nations and the most vigorous economies in the modern world have tended to be democracies. And democracies tend to have legal systems that function independently and reasonably efficiently; for a functioning legal system is, perhaps self-evidently, essential for a market economy. This is as true of the larger countries, notably India and Brazil, as it is of the smaller countries.

And what of the great new economic powerhouse in the East? Many observers of China, some even within China, suggest that the liberalization of the economy and the development of international trade will, almost of necessity, be accompanied over time by a greater measure of political freedom.

7

The European Union today: some achievements

Here I would like to stand back and look at the overall picture: what has the European Union achieved? What are its strengths and its weaknesses? How should it move forward?

The subject is of course very large, but I will concentrate primarily on the aspects of the rule of law and the role of the courts.

There is much that could be said about the achievements of the European Union. There is the single market. The free movement of persons – and not least the free movement of students, able to study in other Member States: a great asset on many counts. There are the achievements of many Community policies: the environmental policy; social policy; greater progress towards equal rights for men and women than would have been achieved nationally. Other policies have been less successful from a UK vantage point, although some might seek to defend them: the common agricultural policy and the common fisheries policy. There is the capacity of the Union to take a collective position in international negotiations, where it has far more influence than the Member States would have individually.

These are certainly significant achievements – not to mention the broader goals of peace and prosperity over a period of more than half a century.

From our present viewpoint, in terms of the rule of

law, we see a Union based on law – indeed there is no other basis available. And a Union whose Member States have agreed not to submit their disputes to any form of settlement other than those prescribed by the Treaties; and whose citizens can also invoke their legal rights before the courts of the Member States.

I would suggest, however, a particular way of looking at the achievements of the European Union.

To see what the European Union has achieved, it seems to me helpful to look at its role first as a magnet – attracting almost the whole of Europe to join it; and then as a model – even for regions outside Europe.

Let us take these in turn.

The European Union as a magnet

When the Six – the founding Member States – drew up the EEC Treaty fifty years ago, they added at the end of the preamble an invitation to other nations to join them, in the following words:

> Resolved by thus pooling their resources to preserve and strengthen peace and liberty, *and calling upon the other peoples of Europe who share their ideal to join in their efforts.*[1]

The Community was never a closed club; rather the contrary, as the preamble suggests and has been the experience. Article 237 of the original EEC Treaty provided: 'Any European State may apply to become a member of the

---

[1] Emphasis added.

Community.' Over the years, virtually every European State has had the ambition to join the Community – now the European Union. To date, in addition to the original Six, twenty-one have done so, in a period of over thirty years, from 1973 to 2007.

The story of the EU's progressive enlargement is in itself remarkable. The story is not widely known, and there is a risk that it is taken for granted. There is much to be learned from it. The story has unfolded in successive stages, with a somewhat different flavour at each stage.

The first enlargement (1973): from six to nine

The EEC Treaty was signed in Rome on 25 March 1957 and the EEC started life on 1 January 1958 with six Member States: Belgium, France, Germany, Italy, Luxembourg and the Netherlands.

They were joined, fifteen years later, by Denmark, Ireland and the United Kingdom – largely, it should be emphasized, for pragmatic, primarily economic reasons, rather than for political or ideological reasons. Nevertheless those new Member States must be taken to have accepted, by joining the European Economic Community, a far higher degree of economic and even political integration than they had envisaged under the much looser European Free Trade Area which they had set up, with four other States (three of which were later to join the European Union) as an alternative or attempted counter to the European Union.

Such a degree of economic integration, and even more political integration, could be regarded as requiring a

Community based on the rule of law and requiring, in particular, an effective judicial system.

The second and third enlargements (1981 and 1986): from nine to twelve

The second and third enlargements were very different. Greece, Portugal and Spain had recently emerged, in dramatic circumstances, from dictatorships.

In each case, the regime had cut the country off from their natural European associates, and indeed from mainstream European values.

There were of course powerful economic arguments for joining. As well as access to the European market, there was access to European funding: money which, on a very large scale, especially in the case of Spain (and correspondingly for an earlier entrant, Ireland), transformed the domestic economy.

It should be noted in passing that the influx of funds benefited not only the domestic economy but, by stimulating investment, growth and demand, also the European economy: an example, not unusual in market economies, of a 'win-win' game.

But over and above the mercantile considerations, these enlargements were of political importance, both symbolic and real. They were designed to recognize and guarantee the transition to democracy and to underpin a liberal regime based not only on an open market economy but also on the rule of law and human rights. Accession can be said to have marked a profound political commitment on both sides.

The fourth enlargement (1995): from twelve to fifteen

The fourth enlargement demonstrates in a different, but no less striking, way the role of the European Union as a magnet. The new Member States, Austria, Finland and Sweden, were in a very different situation both from the former dictatorships which joined in the second and third enlargements and from the former subjects of the Soviet Union which were to join in the fifth and sixth enlargements.

The three new Member States which joined in 1995 were prosperous, stable democracies which had originally chosen to remain outside the European Community, as mentioned, in a much looser European Free Trade Area (EFTA). Indeed they were in the process of negotiating a permanent new relationship with the European Union specifically designed as an alternative to membership: the European Economic Area, which would comprise the twelve EU Member States on the one side and the seven EFTA States on the other and which would give the EFTA States many of the benefits of the European internal market without the political constraints (or 'loss of sovereignty') entailed by EU membership.

Those negotiations were under way when first Austria, then Finland and Sweden, decided to apply to join the European Union instead. They duly joined in 1995. The Governments of Norway and Switzerland sought to join also, but the referendums held in those countries were unsuccessful. The outcome in practice for States which have failed to join is not so fortunate in terms of democracy, even if the outcome is determined by popular vote in a referendum. As is often pointed out, rules agreed by the European Union are routinely accepted in Norway, for example, without its Government, still less its Parliament, having any say in the content of those rules.

In the result, the European Economic Area now comprises only Norway, Iceland and Liechtenstein alongside a European Union of twenty-seven States. Switzerland has stayed outside the European Economic Area; but it has negotiated instead, through a series of agreements, a very close relationship with the European Union. Remarkably, it is now more closely integrated in some fields (even certain fields regarded as central to sovereignty, such as immigration policy) than certain EU Member States.

The fifth and sixth enlargements (2004 and 2007): from fifteen to twenty-seven

The fifth enlargement of the European Union, embracing eight of the countries of central and eastern Europe, as well as Cyprus and Malta, was the most remarkable of all. For more than forty years, since the end of the Second World War and as part of that war's terrible legacy, most of these eight countries had formed part of the Soviet empire, economic freedom extinguished under a system of State control, political freedom suppressed by all the apparatus of the police State.

The fall of the Berlin Wall on 9 November 1989, only fifteen years before this enlargement, symbolized, in the most dramatic way possible, the collapse of the Communist ideology and the end of any challenge to the economic and political model of western Europe.

Indeed it may not be over-dramatic to recall, as Chris Patten has suggested, the scene in Beethoven's opera *Fidelio* in which the prisoners stagger into the light, dazzled by freedom (*Mir ist so wunderbar*). In any event the fall of the Wall marked, in effect, the final stage in the emergence of those countries first from Nazi, then from Soviet tyranny.

Again it was freedom under the law, and freedom guaranteed by law, which was the keystone of enlargement. Look at the conditions for new Member States laid down by the European Union at the Copenhagen Council in 1993, known as the Copenhagen criteria, but which simply codified the existing values of the European Union.

They put as the first requirement:

> That the candidate country has achieved stability of institutions guaranteeing democracy, the rule of law, human rights and respect for and protection of minorities.

Next to that came the economic conditions: the existence of a functioning market economy, and the capacity to cope with competitive pressures and market forces within the Union.

We have already looked at the market aspect, at the values associated with a free economy, and at the functions of the law in this process. I have suggested that the two sets of values are interrelated: that there is an interlocking between the values associated with the rule of law, on the one hand, and the idea of a fully functioning market economy, on the other.

The conditions required of acceding States also included the capacity of the candidate country 'to take on the obligations of membership, including adhering to the aims of political, economic and monetary union'.

What is most striking about the fifth and sixth enlargements, compared with the previous ones, is that, because of the situation of the applicant countries of central and eastern Europe, the enlargement process entailed as a pre-condition of entry the total transformation of the economy, the political structure and it may even be said the very society of those nations.

What this meant in practice was a massive programme of reform: of the economy; of the environment; even of the political system.

What interests us most, in the present context, is the transformation that took place in terms of constitutional and legal values.

New constitutions, and Constitutional courts, were established; that was done in part because of concerns about the independence of the ordinary courts – the independence of the courts being perhaps the most fundamental prerequisite of the rule of law.

There remained concerns, right up to the time of their accession in 2007, about the readiness of Bulgaria and Romania, including concerns about the judicial systems. And there were concerns about imposing continuing conditions to be fulfilled after, rather than before, accession. But it must be remembered that, if the European Union appears more tolerant today about conditions for accession, there are two great differences between the current and the earlier enlargements. First, many of the recent new members have had much further to go to fulfil even the basic requirements of membership. Second, the Union which they are joining is today far more developed than in the case of the earlier enlargements and has itself in many fields attained higher standards.

The story of how the prospect of accession to the European Union proved a powerful incentive to achieve radical transformations in its neighbouring nations seems to have neither any precedent in relations between States nor any counterpart elsewhere in the world today.

As to the past, only the reverse process – from liberty to servitude – seems to have been achieved, and that by a process of armed conquest and subjugation.

As for today's world, outside the European continent, any hopes that liberal, democratic regimes based on the rule of law might be encouraged beyond the frontiers of Europe by developing economic and other relations have yet to be fulfilled. Comparable techniques have been less successful. Carefully designed strategies in certain African countries, for example, are readily undermined when less scrupulous 'donor' countries are willing to curry favour with dictatorial regimes for short-term benefits to themselves.

I have focused very fully on the progressive enlargement of the European Union because an important part of that remarkable story, very little recognized, has been the spread of the rule of law across the European continent, with the associated values of political stability, democracy and perhaps even peace.

The combination of peace and relative prosperity, within a stable democracy based on the rule of law, has characterized the European Union for fifty years. It has proved an attractive entity to join.

The European Union as a model

Outside Europe, the European Union has been seen as a model which has attracted imitation – imitation being justifiably seen as the sincerest form of flattery.

The progressive integration of economies in other regions of the world has been a salient feature in recent years.

The most significant organizations of regional economic integration include:

- The North American Free Trade Agreement – NAFTA.
- The Association of Southeast Asian Nations – ASEAN.
- Two groupings in Latin America:
  - The Southern [American] Common Market, *Mercado Comun del Sur* or 'Mercosur'; and
  - The Andes Pact.
- Several regional groupings in Africa, including SADC (southern Africa), COMESA (east and southern Africa), ECOWAS (west Africa), etc., with the attempt now being made to form a continent-wide African Union – directly reflecting the European Union.

There are clearly very good reasons for this trend towards transnational economic integration, against a broader background of globalization. Such groups may aim to bring together like-minded countries, and perhaps also countries with some shared values – sometimes reflecting shared cultures, shared languages, etc. Equally, they may aim to develop and to build common values.

But the development of these groups also suggests, at a fundamental level, the growing universal appeal of a particular set of values, of particular interest for our theme: the resolution of disputes by law, by legal process and above all by an independent judiciary.

Increasingly, these organizations seek to resolve disputes by judicial and similar means of settlement.

Although this is a process which has been taken furthest by the European Union, it is not of course unique to the European Union. An outstanding example, on the global level, is the evolution of the dispute-settlement system of the World Trade Organization. This has evolved from a weak system, based on consensus, to a system embodying the essential features of judicial process.

Disputes between States over international trade now feature compulsory jurisdiction; disputes are settled by applying rules of law; decisions are binding on the parties; sanctions can be imposed if decisions are not observed.

But although the trend towards judicial settlement is a general one, it is significant that several regional organizations have based, or sought to base, their system very closely on the specific features of the EU system, and have explicitly taken that system, and specifically the judicial system embodied in the European Court of Justice (ECJ), as their template.

Perhaps I could take three examples from my own experience. My first example of the power of the ECJ model is from Moscow.

Russia: the European Union and the Kremlin

In 1991 extraordinary changes were taking place in the Soviet Union, and the repercussions reached the ECJ in

Luxembourg. We received a visit from the Soviet Minister of Justice, who told us in the course of our discussions that he had come to learn. He added that he had brought a large empty suitcase from Moscow, because he wanted to take back with him many books on the ECJ. Having co-authored (with Professor Neville Brown) a short book on the Court, I supplied a copy. I then received a series of friendly visits from officials from the Soviet Embassy in Luxembourg, who had many questions for me. Above all, they asked, what is meant by the rule of law?

When I explained what I understood by the rule of law, they said: 'Ah yes, we had something like that in Russia once, very briefly: it was in 1905' – no doubt a reference to the short-lived Revolution of that year.

I then, at their request, wrote for them a note on the rule of law.

The next step was an invitation to visit Moscow for a conference of the States making up the Soviet Union, just before Christmas 1991: as it turned out, the last days of the Soviet Union, and the last days in power of President Mikhail Gorbachev. The conference took place in the Kremlin, in the building housing his offices (just next door to the conference room), as it had previously housed those of Lenin, Stalin and others. The conference room itself was a grand oval chamber, which I was told had been the Russian headquarters in the Second World War.

The object of the conference – masterminded by Gorbachev's legal adviser, Vinyamin Yakovlev – was no less than to replace the Soviet Union with a Community of independent States modelled on the European Community and based on the rule of law. It was to have a Court of Justice modelled on the ECJ, and it was my job (as the sole outsider at the conference) to explain to the delegates (in English, with consecutive interpretation) the role and functions of the ECJ.

One of the extraordinary features of the conference was that the delegates came not only from the more dependent constituent States of the Soviet Union, including the Islamic States, but also from the Baltic States – Estonia, Latvia and Lithuania – which had already achieved some measure of independence and some years later were to join the European Union.

These Baltic States, despite their relatively advanced political culture, and their ardent desire to escape the grip of the Soviet bear, were ready to contemplate voluntary accession to a Community of States, established by the Soviet Union, but based not upon force, but upon the rule of law. There were high hopes of the new Community.

It was not to be. A few days later, on 25 December 1991, Gorbachev resigned. Although his successor as President, Boris Yeltsin, had favoured the broad idea of a Community with a Court, the plan never materialized.

What emerged instead was the Commonwealth of Independent States.[2] But there was no court; and many would add, no rule of law.

---

[2] The Commonwealth of Independent States (CIS) (in Russian: СоДружество Неэависимых ГосуДарств (СНГ) – *Sodruzhestvo Nezavisimykh Gosudarstv*) is the international organization, or alliance, consisting of eleven former Soviet Republics: Armenia, Azerbaijan, Belarus, Georgia, Kazakhstan, Kyrgyzstan, Moldova, Russia, Tajikistan, Ukraine and Uzbekistan. Turkmenistan discontinued permanent membership as of 26 August 2005 and is now an associate member.

Africa: the Southern African Development Community and the African Union

The second example is from Africa: I was asked to advise the Southern African Development Community (SADC) on the establishment of a Court of Justice. That Community comprises most of the States of southern Africa and has played a significant political role in recent years.

The advice was to be based on the experience, or experiments, of such courts throughout the world, but it was clear that the leading model was to be the ECJ. The Statute of a Court of Justice was duly drawn up, although I confess that it departed in significant respects from my proposals.

This is by no means the only court of its type in Africa. Several other regional organizations have established courts closely modelled on the ECJ. In particular, they make provision for the key mechanism of references from the courts of their member States to a central court for a ruling on questions of law arising under their respective treaties.

The African Union, replacing the Organisation of African Union and extending to the whole continent of Africa, is modelled in part on the European Union. Certainly it is less

Footnote 2 (cont.)

The creation of the CIS signalled the dissolution of the Soviet Union and, according to Russian leaders, its purpose was to 'allow a civilized divorce' between the Soviet Republics. However, many observers perceive the CIS as a geopolitical tool, allowing Russia to maintain its influence over the former Soviet republics. Since its formation, the member States of the CIS have signed a large number of documents concerning integration and cooperation on matters of economics, defence and foreign policy.

ambitious in its institutional and legal dimensions. The founding instrument, the Constitutive Act of the African Union, dated 11 July 2000, does, however, provide for a Court of Justice. The Protocol establishing the Statute of the Court of Justice was signed three years later, on 11 July 2003. It is to have, initially at least, limited functions compared with the ECJ (what court does not?), but there is a possibility that its jurisdiction will be expanded in an interesting direction.

In my proposals for the Court of Justice of SADC, I had included what might have seemed a revolutionary idea: that the SADC Court should not only have jurisdiction over the 'development' matters which fell directly within the competence of the organization, but also an embryonic form of human rights jurisdiction. The idea was not accepted. However, I was interested to discover, when preparing these lectures, that a similar idea has gained ground within the African Union.

It is apparently envisaged that the 'African Court of Justice' to be set up in the African Union will at some point in the future be merged with the African Court on Human and Peoples' Rights and be the African Union's legal organ. The new Court will have responsibility both for human rights and for the future African Economic Community.

The Caribbean Court of Justice

Finally I must mention, all too briefly, the Caribbean Court of Justice, which I look forward to visiting shortly. It too was closely modelled on the ECJ, and I have been invited to address them on the experience of the European Court.

There are two main aspects of the jurisdiction of the Caribbean Court of Justice. It sits as the final court of appeal for the Caribbean States which have accepted that jurisdiction, thus replacing the Judicial Committee of the Privy Council. And it has a jurisdiction modelled on that of the ECJ on economic issues for all the States forming the Caribbean Economic Community. Here too, the model of the European Union and the ECJ has proved attractive.

8

The European Union today: some problems

So far I have concentrated on some of the strengths of the European project. Now I should like to look at some of the concerns that have been expressed, and some of the questions that arise.

I will take three: loss of sovereignty, excessive regulation and over-ambition. All have some relation to the overall theme of the rule of law.

The loss of sovereignty

The concern over loss of sovereignty has, I suggest, some dubious aspects, but others which are better founded.

The notion of the sovereign State is outmoded. It has been replaced, I would suggest, by two main ideas. First, there is now, and increasingly, an allocation of powers, which are divided, in different realms, among different levels of government: local, national, regional, global. This is true, very obviously, in political terms, but it is also increasingly true in legal terms.

In legal terms, the last word, on certain matters of international security, now rests with the United Nations Security Council; on many aspects of international trade, with the World Trade Organization and its Court (the 'Appellate Body'). In Europe, the last word on human rights is often for the European Court of Human Rights; the last word on the European internal market is for the European Court of Justice.

Second, the formerly sovereign States can effectively act jointly by sharing their powers. There are advantages today in thinking in terms of 'powers' rather than 'sovereignty'. Powers can be shared, whereas it is difficult to think of shared sovereignty.

And there are obvious advantages in sharing powers in particular fields. The world has moved on since the European Economic Community was founded fifty years ago. In many, and apparently ever more, fields action is needed on the international level. It can be achieved only by the painful, but often productive, process of negotiation. The European Union collectively can obviously achieve more in international negotiations than the Member States could achieve individually.

Many aspects of State action do not fall within national frontiers: not only international trade in goods and services, but many markets: financial markets, energy markets and others. The protection of the environment and the conservation of natural resources cannot sensibly be left any longer to 'sovereign' States.

Then there is the perennial problem of democratic control. Where powers are shared between States, such control, historically based on national Parliaments, may be more difficult.

But democratic control has not operated, even within the unitary State, as well as might be assumed by those concerned.

Indeed the notions of sovereignty and democracy are not natural bedfellows at all. Within the United Kingdom, the supposed combination of sovereignty and democracy has often amounted to a Parliament controlled by an apparently all-powerful executive government – what Lord Hailsham described as an elective dictatorship. At the present time, the current Government's respect for the wishes of the electorate sometimes seems to translate into a legislative logjam responding to little more than the need for the Government to be seen to be active – even if only by reaction to so-called 'focus groups', or even to the latest headlines in the tabloid Press.

In the European Union, the European Parliament is inevitably – because of the size of the Union, with a population now of around 500 million – extremely remote from the electorate; the same is no doubt true of the largest democracies everywhere, and especially perhaps in India and the United States. Yet the European Parliament now exercises far greater control and influence over the content of European legislation than the national Parliaments of almost all, and perhaps all, the Member States can exercise over domestic legislation. None the less, it may be desirable for national Parliaments to have some greater measure of influence on European legislation.

What is most valid in concerns of this kind is the concern about the exercise of the European Union's competences in areas where the case for European action is not fully made out. The line is a very difficult one to draw; but could more be done to reinforce the frontier? This is not strictly an issue of sovereignty, since we are looking at a system of shared powers. But we return to the point when we look at regulation.

Excessive interference/excessive regulation

This issue is a constant refrain in the European Union: there are constant complaints about too much regulation from Brussels, too much interference from the ECJ in Luxembourg.

Such complaints are not always, of course, disinterested. Industry and commerce, for example, are sometimes not well disposed to regulation, which they claim harms efficiency and competitiveness. But others may have, from a different point of view, a more favourable attitude to regulation. To them, much of the regulation may seem desirable to protect the interests of employees, or to protect their health, or to ensure the safety of their products, or to comply with international agreements or to guarantee financial probity. Regulation may be needed, not to regulate this well-run company, but to regulate other less well-run companies.

Sometimes the main object of criticism is not regulation in itself, but the fact that it emanates from Brussels. Of course that may make regulation less responsive to domestic concerns, so that the outcome may seem worse.

There are several strands in the reply to such objections. First, undue interference is not a prerogative of European regulation: domestic regulation also often seems excessive and exorbitant, especially in the United Kingdom under the all-pervasive 'health and safety' culture, which sometimes now verges on the absurd. Have you tried recently to get a licence to serve a glass of wine in your village hall?

Second, we are looking at trade, which is increasingly global, and where the aim is to create and manage a single

140

market, at least in Europe. Most regulation does not touch individuals at all. And often regulation is for the benefit of the traders. Indeed, it may be better to have a single EU-wide regime, even an imperfect one, rather than a separate system, perhaps frequently modified, not always easy to ascertain, for each of the twenty-seven Member States of the European Union.

Regulation is essential to remove barriers to trade. It may seem at first sight a paradox, but it is obvious that free markets depend to a substantial degree upon regulation.

Nevertheless of course there should be the most intense scrutiny politically, and even some degree of scrutiny judicially, of whether a proposed measure is necessary, or whether it is necessary in all its detail, or whether it should be adopted as a European measure or could be left, under the principle of subsidiarity, to the Member States.

On the political level, there was a welcome provision in the European Constitutional Treaty for assessing compliance with the principle of subsidiarity. It would have given national Parliaments an important role in the process, and the possibility of blocking measures in advance.

Was this idea lost with the Constitution, or could it be revived, if only informally, so that the Commission would be required to reconsider proposals for legislation, or would do so voluntarily, where, for example, three or more national Parliaments objected to the proposal, and in doing so would take full account of the concerns of the national Parliaments?

And the ECJ could perhaps play a larger role. By construing less broadly the competences of the European Union and by taking a more strict view of subsidiarity.

Over-ambition

The European Constitution

In 2005 the Constitutional Treaty was rejected in referendums – first in France, then in the Netherlands.

In the United Kingdom the rejection of the Treaty in the two referendums may have been greeted with a variety of reactions, ranging from rejoicing to relief. But it is worth considering reactions elsewhere.

Indeed the Treaty is still worth examining. The Treaty, the reasons for its adoption, the processes by which it was adopted and rejected and the reasons for its rejection, have valuable lessons for us.

We should bear in mind, first of all, that the Treaty represented a huge investment of intellectual and political capital. Notwithstanding attempts to portray it as merely a tidying-up exercise, as if it were simply sorting out some of the mess left by earlier treaties, it was an ambitious – perhaps an over-ambitious – exercise. And there is much that we risk forgetting. Not merely that the Treaty was accepted by the Governments of all twenty-five Member States – remarkable though that is. Not merely that most of them have ratified it – in a number of cases after positive referendum results. And not merely that the Treaty contained, as I shall suggest, a number of very positive features – indeed, features which should have been welcomed in all camps, by 'Europhiles' and 'Europhobes' alike.

All these points are important, but what is perhaps most important is to understand the reasons why there was a call for a constitutional treaty in the first place, and why these underlying concerns are likely to remain, whatever the future holds. It is necessary to grasp these matters if there is to be a meaningful discussion on the future of the Constitution, or indeed on the future of the European Union itself.

The need for a Constitution?

It is helpful to understand why objections of principle to the very idea of a constitution are rather weak. One objection, frequently voiced in the United Kingdom, is that a constitution implies a State, and that a constitution, for the European Union implies a super-State. That kind of objection seems to overestimate what is meant by a constitution. As is often pointed out, many bodies other than States have constitutions: bodies ranging from international organizations to golf clubs.

Moreover, the objection seems to underestimate what the European Union already is: a Union in which competences are divided between the Union and the Member States, and in which Union measures and Union law necessarily prevail over State measures. It is a Union based on law. The first, incidentally, of its kind: a union of independent States, and one based not on military force or on diplomatic manoeuvrings, but on law.

Such objections to a constitution also underestimate how the Union is seen in political and legal circles in other Member States. It is seen as the basis for much of the domestic and foreign policy of the State. The exercise of vital powers is based on treaties concluded by democratic governments. But the exercise of those powers is not seen as subject to sufficient controls. Many of the Member States can now be said to share a degree of constitutional traditions – relatively recent and even intermittent though they may be in historical terms. Fundamental constitutional principles require that powers be exercised with respect for human rights; that they be exercised in accordance with democratic principles; that they be subject to judicial review.

Those principles also underlie, of course, the constitution of the United Kingdom, even though the notion of a UK constitution still sounds strange to our ears, and even though the notion of constitutionalism is only now gaining ground here.

But it can also be argued that the need for a constitution for the European Union is greater even than is a constitution for the Member States. Since competences are exercised by the European Union and its institutions directly; since the European Union has what are traditionally the three branches of government, in that those institutions have wide-ranging legislative, executive and judicial powers, it becomes even more important that those powers should be exercised within defined limits and in accordance with accepted constitutional principles.

It is true that it has been possible to regard the European Union as already having a constitution of a sort: namely, the founding Treaties, as interpreted by the ECJ, which has indeed over the years interpreted the EC Treaty, in particular, in a fashion appropriate to the interpretation of a constitution. In a famous passage I have already quoted, the ECJ was able to say that the Community 'is a Community based on the rule of law, inasmuch as neither its Member States nor its institutions can avoid a review of the question whether the measures adopted by them are in conformity with the basic constitutional charter, the Treaty'.

The ECJ thus combined, in the *Les Verts* case,[1] three powerful notions: a constitution, a Community based on the rule of law, and a complete system of remedies.

The jurisdiction of the European Court of Justice – the three pillars

The *Les Verts* case was decided twenty years ago, in what can now be seen, in terms of the jurisdiction of the ECJ, as a halcyon age. That was when the Court's jurisdiction was broadly comprehensive. It was before the Maastricht Treaty introduced the so-called three-pillar structure, which largely confined the jurisdiction of the ECJ to the first, 'Community', pillar, with virtually no jurisdiction under the second pillar (Common Foreign and Security Policy) and very limited jurisdiction under the third pillar (Justice and Home Affairs).

There was some extension of jurisdiction in relation to these matters a few years later under the Amsterdam Treaty, but only at the price of greater confusion. Matters relating to asylum, immigration and certain other questions were transferred to the 'Community' pillar, but with different, and sometimes optional, provisions on the jurisdiction of the ECJ.

So there is now a whole range of different regimes in relation to very similar areas, even excluding the rather separate second pillar: there is the traditional Community regime;

---

[1] *Parti Ecologiste Les Verts* v. *European Parliament* [1986] ECR 1339.

the variants on that regime for first-pillar matters transferred by Amsterdam; and the revised third pillar regime.

There is now far greater uncertainty about the borderline between these regimes than there was with the previous dividing line between the first and third pillars. The net result is both to limit in an apparently random way the jurisdiction of the ECJ and to create apparently maximal confusion about its scope.

These developments are particularly regrettable given the incontestable fact that what has proved the key to the development of the Community legal order has been the jurisdiction of the ECJ. Perhaps paradoxically, it can almost be said that the basic all-encompassing provisions of the original EEC Treaty conferring jurisdiction on the Court have proved more important than its substantive provisions. And incidentally that is why, in assessing what needs to be done to reform the European Union, and particularly in considering the future of the Constitutional Treaty, it is appropriate to look in the first place at the Court's jurisdiction.

There is a further paradox in limiting the ECJ's jurisdiction under the third pillar, in particular, which is concerned with matters fundamental to the rights of the individual, especially in relation to criminal law and criminal procedure.

It is true that the ECJ has striven, as in the *Pupino* case,[2] to remedy some of the great lacunae thus opened up.

But a proper solution to the patchwork created by successive ill-thought-out Treaty amendments can now be found only by a full-scale recasting of the Treaty, removing the unfortunate three-pillar structure.

---

[2] *Pupino (criminal proceedings against)* [2005] ECR I-5285.

This is indeed one of the features, and one of the great merits, of the Constitutional Treaty. And although it would still restrict the jurisdiction of the ECJ, it would do so in a less arbitrary fashion.

Human rights and the Constitutional Treaty

It is appropriate to turn next to the protection of human rights in the legal order of the European Union. Here the Constitutional Treaty would make two major innovations. First, it would introduce, as Part II of the Constitution, the EU's own Charter of Fundamental Rights. Second, it would provide for accession by the Union to the European Convention on Human Rights. It would thus entail, with the necessary institutional modifications, acceptance by the European Union of the jurisdiction of the Strasbourg Court; so making possible a direct challenge to Luxembourg in Strasbourg.

What are we to make of these innovations? To examine them, we must briefly recall the background.

As we have seen, the Community Treaties themselves contained – and still contain – no list of human rights; but the gaps have once again been substantially, if not completely, filled by the case-law of the ECJ. The Court has relied both on the European Convention on Human Rights (although the European Union is not a party to the Convention) and on the fundamental rights provisions contained in the national Constitutions of the Member States, or embodied in their con-stitutional traditions. These provisions on fundamental rights the Court has accepted as 'general principles of law'.

The formula on human rights finally introduced by the Amsterdam Treaty in 1997 was based verbatim on the ECJ's case-law and, in effect, constitutionalized it.

By Article 6(2) of the EC Treaty, as thus amended: 'The Union shall respect fundamental rights, as guaranteed by the [European Convention on Human Rights] and as they result from the constitutional traditions common to the Member States, as general principles of Community law.'

As to the Charter of Fundamental Rights, this was adopted by the European Union in 2000. But as yet the Charter has no legal force. The ECJ in its judgments has so far placed no reliance on it, and while the Advocates General (and indeed the Court of First Instance) have referred to it, these references generally suggest that the Charter is a non-binding source of the scope of those human rights provisions which are recognized in the Member States.

Let us come back to the Charter shortly.

Then there is the idea, embodied in the Constitutional Treaty, that the European Union should become a party to the European Convention on Human Rights. That would require, in addition, significant amendments to the Convention.

I confess to some hesitation over that idea, but it seems to have been almost universally accepted, if sometimes for reasons of appearance rather than substance. It has been described as of symbolic importance; it might indeed have at least some cosmetic value.

There are many good features of the Constitutional Treaty. Some of them are largely political, and need no discussion here.

For example, there is the new voting system in the Council, clearly a better system than that adopted in the Nice Treaty, and reflecting a fairer balance between the Member States. There is the better provision for a longer-term presidency of the European Union, and arguably better provision for the external representation of the Union in foreign affairs.

There is the more detailed catalogue of the European Union's competences, in an attempt to demarcate more clearly the competences of the Union and those of the Member States.

And in that connection, the Constitution seeks to reinforce observance of the principle of subsidiarity.

One potentially important innovation in the Constitutional Treaty is to give national Parliaments a greater role on subsidiarity. The principle of giving national Parliaments a greater role, both in practice and symbolically, may be worthwhile, especially in this context.

There will always be concern about the 'democratic deficit' in the European Union – often leading to calls for the European Parliament's powers to be increased – even if that concern sometimes seems exaggerated: after all, the ministers of the Member States are subject to democratic control in their national systems; and the European Parliament already seems to have appreciably more power than the national Parliaments of at least some of the Member States. But no doubt perceptions here are also important, and the European Union has a special need for legitimacy.

And substance is important too. We can appreciate the value of giving national Parliaments more say, in particular, in the assessment of subsidiarity. Perhaps this mechanism for involving the national Parliaments, or some variant of it, could be used in practice, without the need for a Treaty amendment.

Indeed some of the most fundamental ideas of the Constitutional Treaty might perhaps form the basis of unwritten rules, or even constitutional conventions, perhaps reflected in informal agreements between the Council and the Parliament, and where appropriate the national Parliaments and the Commission.

I have mentioned several valuable, or even very valuable, features of the Constitutional Treaty. But I have to say that there are also grave defects, and despite its merits, and despite the huge amount invested in it, it is difficult to accept that it is the right solution.

One grave defect is that it contains too much.

It would have been far better if the Constitution had been limited to the provisions which are genuinely constitutional. They are mainly contained in Part I of the Treaty. Indeed it was not only unnecessary, but a move in the wrong direction, to include in the Constitution the substantive provisions of the EC Treaty, and so to upgrade them all and give them constitutional status.

On the contrary, since many of those provisions are not of constitutional importance, they could well have been downgraded and so made more easily amendable. Instead, they have been carved in stone, even granite. And they have made the Constitution wholly unwieldy, a colossus. I repeat, it contains too much.

And it promises too much: more, in some instances, than it is likely to deliver. Here I think especially of the Charter of Fundamental Rights, agreed in 2000 but now constituting

Part II of the Constitution. It may have seemed a good idea, some years ago, for the European Union to have its own Charter of Rights, suited to its own competences, and expressing its own values, but the Charter as it emerges in Part II of the Constitutional Treaty is unsatisfactory in several respects.

To mention briefly some main points:

1. Certain provisions of the Charter are intended to do no more than reproduce the rights set out in the European Convention on Human Rights: but they express them in a different form and in different language, which seems a recipe for confusion.
2. The Charter includes both judicially enforceable rights, like the Convention rights, and other rights, social or economic, which in some respects are not obviously justiciable.
3. Rights apparently proclaimed without qualification in the Charter would have to be understood in the light of 'explanations' – the qualifications added during the negotiations – which significantly reduce their scope.
4. Contrary to first impressions, the Charter is not an all-purpose human rights instrument for the European Union. It is addressed only to the EU institutions, and to the Member States only when they are implementing EU law. This limit is likely to cause much confusion; and indeed the intended borderline is not always easy to draw.

Above all, the Charter is likely to disappoint expectations: to deliver less than it promises.

The founding Treaties, in contrast, perhaps had the merit that they delivered what they promised, and sometimes more.

Conclusions

The concerns about loss of sovereignty and over-regulation need to be addressed. Better informed discussion and debate are needed; they can help better decision-making. Where there are genuine concerns and genuine problems, they are far from insoluble. On the broadest level, there needs to be recognition that, as the European Union becomes more effective, it can also become rather more relaxed in some areas of its activity.

The European Union can also be better focused. Political leaders have come forward with rather grandiose ideas. In some ways, their over-ambition can be seen positively, as a recognition of the success of the European project and of its significance. But they have sometimes failed in more mundane activities, perhaps especially in liberalizing their markets. Instead, they have too often tried to fix labour markets, to maintain 'national champions', to pursue outmoded industrial policy.

There are indications, however, that the European Union is adapting to new requirements. The priorities, alongside the continuing need for economic liberalization, are in areas such as energy and the environment. Fortunately, there is increasing recognition of these priorities.

It seems beyond dispute that these are now areas where the Member States cannot act unilaterally: European solutions are necessary.

Afterword

We have seen in this book how new tasks are imposed on the courts. The functions of law have changed in recent years. Courts must now, for example, seek to strike the balance where competing values conflict. They have a role in developing policy as well as in settling disputes.

At first sight it may seem that the courts are not well placed to respond to these challenges, which go well beyond deciding the instant case. Traditionally, courts are, for the most part, concerned with deciding individual cases – although the task of the European Court of Justice, in giving preliminary rulings, can be seen to have a broader significance. Under this procedure, its rulings are intended, not only to resolve the issue arising in the instant case, but also to settle the matter for all courts in the European Union confronted with the same questions.

It can also be argued that fundamental choices should be made by a democratically accountable legislature, rather than by the courts. But our survey has shown, I think, that that is not always a workable solution. Courts will always be left with the last word.

To a large extent, the courts' new tasks are unavoidable. But they also have the advantage of new methods of addressing the issues.

One is through dialogue between courts in different systems: they look at each other's decisions far more than in the past. They decide explicitly whether solutions adopted elsewhere are appropriate in their own systems.

In addition, there is greater scrutiny and analysis of court decisions by academic lawyers; and greater recognition of their input by the courts. There is happily no longer a rule – which apparently once prevailed in England – that a legal scholar could be cited in court only after his death.

In Europe, these benefits are very well developed. There is, as we have seen, greater dialogue between courts. On the academic front, a truly European scholarship has been built up.

Moreover a truly European judicial system has grown up, with two complementary branches, the European Community branch and the European Convention on Human Rights. By a combination of history, political impetus, chance and design, the two branches have developed, independently yet interactively; and the European experience has attracted interest and indeed admiration worldwide.

To continue to develop healthily, the European judicial system needs to be under constant scrutiny. It can only benefit from academic criticism, from dialogue with other judges, and from informed public debate.

My hope is that future Hamlyn lecturers will take this process further: there could in my view be no better way of fulfilling Emma Hamlyn's wishes.